THE HISTORY OF POKER
The Origins, Evolution, Facts and Trivia of Poker

KEN WARREN

authorHOUSE®

AuthorHouse™
1663 Liberty Drive
Bloomington, IN 47403
www.authorhouse.com
Phone: 1-800-839-8640

First published by AuthorHouse 6/29/2010

ISBN: 978-1-4490-1137-6 (sc)

Printed in the United States of America
Bloomington, Indiana

This book is printed on acid-free paper.

OTHER BOOKS BY KEN WARREN

Winner's Guide to Texas Hold'em Poker, 1996, ISBN: 0-940685-59-0

Winner's Guide to Omaha Poker, 2003, ISBN: 1-58042-102-4

Ken Warren Teaches Texas Hold'em, Vol 1, 2003, ISBN: 1-58042-085-0

The Big Book of Poker, 2004, ISBN: 1-58042-113-X

Ken Warren Teaches 7-Card Stud, 2008, ISBN: 1-58042-221-7

Ken Warren Teaches Texas Hold'em, Vol 2, 2008, ISBN: 1-58042-254-3

DEDICATION

It is with a deep sense of appreciation and with a grateful heart that I enthusiastically dedicate this book to Howard and Marjie Wilson of Durango, Colorado. This book could not have been published in the time and manner that it was without their support, their belief in me and their interest in history. Sometimes in life you get dealt a bad hand, you sometimes break even and you even get to win a few hands once in a while. When I met Howard and Marjie it was as if life had dealt me a royal flush that I get to take with me to every game for the rest of my life. Thanks, Howard and Marjie for helping change my life like you have.

I also owe an inestimable debt to Ralph Wetterhahn of Long Beach, California for being an inspiration to me, for believing in me, for being there when needed and always being there when not needed. Thanks Ralph, for teaching me the true meaning of John 13:34.

I also want to recognize the contributions of my good friend Bob Creek of Maryland Park (St. Charles) Missouri. His ideas, editorial contributions and sharp eye for detail helped make this book the quality product that it is.

THE TIMELINE OF THE HISTORY OF POKER

TABLE OF CONTENTS

Chapter 1
The Early History of Playing Cards…6
The Earliest Betting and Bluffing-Type Card Games…8
The Origins of American-Style Poker…17

Chapter 2
1970 World Series of Poker, Johnny Moss…46

Chapter 3
1971 World Series of Poker, Johnny Moss…47

Chapter 4
1972 World Series of Poker, Thomas "Amarillo Slim" Preston…48

Chapter 5
1973 World Series of Poker, Walter Clyde "Puggy" Pearson…49

Chapter 6
1974 World Series of Poker, Johnny Moss…52

Chapter 7
1975 World Series of Poker, Brian "Sailor" Roberts…53

Chapter 8
1976 World Series of Poker, Doyle "Texas Dolly" Brunson…54

Chapter 9
1977 World Series of Poker, Doyle "Texas Dolly" Brunson…56

Chapter 10
1978 World Series of Poker, Bobby "The Owl" Baldwin…58

Chapter 11
1979 World Series of Poker, Hal Fowler…60

Chapter 12
1980 World Series of Poker, Stuart "The Kid" Ungar...63

Chapter 13
1981 World Series of Poker, Stuart "The Kid" Ungar...65

Chapter 14
1982 World Series of Poker, Jack "Treetop" Straus...67

Chapter 15
1983 World Series of Poker, Tom McEvoy...69

Chapter 16
1984 World Series of Poker, "Gentleman" Jack Keller...72

Chapter 17
1985 World Series of Poker, Bill Smith...73

Chapter 18
1986 World Series of Poker, Berry Johnston...75

Chapter 19
1987 World Series of Poker, Johnny "The Orient Express" Chan...77

Chapter 20
1988 World Series of Poker, Johnny "The Orient Express" Chan...78

Chapter 21
1989 World Series of Poker, Phil "The Poker Brat" Hellmuth...80

Chapter 22
1990 World Series of Poker, Mansour Matloubi...82

Chapter 23
1991 World Series of Poker, Brad Daugherty...84

Chapter 24
1992 World Series of Poker, Hamid Dastmalchi...85

Chapter 25
1993 World Series of Poker, Jim Bechtel...88

Chapter 26
1994 World Series of Poker, Russ Hamilton...90

Chapter 27
1995 World Series of Poker, "Action" Dan Harrington...91

Chapter 28
1996 World Series of Poker, Huckleberry "Huck" Seed...94

Chapter 29
1997 World Series of Poker, Stuart "The Kid" Ungar...96

Chapter 30
1998 World Series of Poker, Scotty Nguyen...98

Chapter 31
1999 World Series of Poker, J.J. "Noel" Furlong...101

Chapter 32
2000 World Series of Poker, Chris "Jesus" Ferguson...102

Chapter 33
2001 World Series of Poker, Carlos Mortensen...105

Chapter 34
2002 World Series of Poker, Robert Varkonyi...107

Chapter 35
2003 World Series of Poker, Chris Moneymaker...110

Chapter 36
2004 World Series of Poker, Greg Raymer...113

Chapter 37
2005 World Series of Poker, Joe Hachem...116

Chapter 38

2006 World Series of Poker, Jamie Gold…120

Chapter 39
2007 World Series of Poker, Jerry Yang…124

Chapter 40
2008 World Series of Poker, Peter Eastgate…128

Chapter 41
2009 World Series of Poker…136

Appendix I
World Series of Poker All-Time Money Winners…144

Appendix II
Lifetime WSOP Earnings of Each WSOP Champion…144

Appendix III
What the WSOP Championship Winner's List
Would Look
Like if the Runner-up Had Won…145

Appendix IV
Number of WSOP Preliminary Events by Year…146

Appendix V
Interesting WSOP Trivia…147

Appendix VI
Number of Players at Each WSOP Main Event…149

Appendix VII
1st, 2nd, 3rd and 4th Place Prize Money for Each WSOP Main Event…150

Appendix VIII
The Poker Hall of Fame…152

Appendix IX
Women In Poker Hall of Fame…153

INTRODUCTION

This is the part of the book that most everyone skips over when starting to read a book. Even authors skip other author's intros. Yet every book still has an introduction. You'd think that writers would lose interest in writing intros even when they know most readers won't be reading it. So, why am I taking the time and effort to do the work of writing this intro? It's because I know that poker players and folks who are interested in the history if anything are, on average, a lot more intelligent than the rest of the general population. It's because I know that if the title of this book interested you, you'd read the introduction.

I used to teach US History and US Government at Arizona State University in the late 1970's. I learned how to play poker in January of 1981. It was inevitable that these two interests would eventually merge in my mind to become *The History of Poker*. I had a great, fun time doing the research necessary to put all of this together. I specifically designed this book to be a 'light read' to make it more enjoyable than a standard history book or text. It's full of trivia, fun facts, interesting unknown tidbits of American history and some of the historical figures you may not have known were poker players.

When I first decided to write *The History of Poker*, I was faced with the dilemma that has been shared by every historian who ever wanted to write about the history of anything. I naturally wanted to start this book at the beginning but how do you answer the question, "How far back is the beginning?" Did it start with the first World Series of Poker in 1970? Nope. Have to go back further than that. How about the first time 7-Card Stud was played? That's not far enough back because 5-Card Stud was played before that. The first true American-style poker game was a game that was called Whiskey Poker but is actually better described as "5-Card Draw Without the Draw," played as early as the 1820's in New Orleans. But where did that game come from? To explain how that game came into existence, I had to look at betting and bluffing card games that were played in England, France, Spain and Germany for three hundred years before that. *Now*, it appears I've gone back far enough to explain how these games have evolved into the poker game you play and watch on television today.

Then I decided to do one more thing. We don't play poker by mental telepathy, do we? Of course not. I decided to begin this book by explaining how the playing cards we use came into existence. It's a very interesting story. So, this book begins with the evolution of playing cards, introduces the European betting and bluffing games played with them and then follows those games across the Atlantic Ocean where French settlers and American frontiersmen made them their own. This history takes you through the logical creation of 5-Card Stud, 5-Card Draw, 7-Card Stud (more popularly then known as "5-Card Stud With Two Extra Cards"), High-Low Poker, Lowball and Texas Hold'em. Starting with the first World Series of Poker in 1970, I then present you with everything you need to know about every WSOP after that, including the exact cards played (when known), along with some interesting facts to go with it.

I've included as much relevant biographical data as I could find on the most well-known poker players, including personal details about their personalities. I've tried to also make this a poker reference-research book—one that will answer your most common poker questions. What happened in the poker world in 1820, 1905 or 1970? Who won the WSOP in 1983 and who did he beat with which cards? Take a look inside and see for yourself.

Ken Warren
St. Charles, Missouri, July 12, 2009
Kennolga@yahoo.com

THE EARLY HISTORY OF PLAYING CARDS

800s – The earliest known playing cards came from Central Asia, most likely from China or Hindustan. Paper was first made in China around 100 A.D.; therefore it seems most likely that playing cards originated there also.

900s – Paper dominoes were created by the Chinese. They were used like we use modern-day playing cards instead of like we use dominoes.

969, December 31st – The Chinese emperor Mu-tsung played domino cards with his wife.

1100 – One of the earliest known playing cards came from Chinese Turkestan. The suits were coins, clubs, cups and swords.

1100s – Korean playing cards were made of oiled paper about 7 5/8ths inches long and ½ inch wide with a picture of an arrow on the back. There were eight suits: men, fish, crows, pheasants, antelopes, stars, rabbits and horses. There were ten cards of each suit, making a deck of eighty cards.

1190 – An edict issued by the Court of Richard the Lionhearted said,

> "No person in the army is permitted to play at any sort of game
> except knights and clergymen; who in one whole day and night
> shall not, each, lose more than twenty schillings on pain of
> forfeiting 100 schillings to the archbishop of the army".

This is the first known mention of money management, even though the advice carried the weight of law.

1210 – The earliest known European playing cards were copied from the Chinese cards.

1200s – Playing cards in India used a different bright color on the backs of the cards to indicate the different suits.

1299 – Playing cards were introduced into Italy.

1370 – Scholars are adamant that playing cards did not exist anywhere else in Europe besides Italy prior to this date. The best available evidence that this is probably true is the fact that Petrarch (1307-74), Boccaccio (1313-75) and Chaucer (1343-1400) do not mention playing cards at all in any of their works. Also, Guillaume de Machau's address to Charles V in 1364 which vehemently denounced gaming in general, and dice in particular, does not mention playing cards. Additionally, city ordinances from St. Gallen (1364) and Paris (1369) make no mention of playing cards.

1371 – Playing cards were introduced into Spain. They're mentioned in a Catalan document and referred to as naip. The current Spanish spelling is naipes.

1377 – Playing cards were introduced into Switzerland.

1377 – The first known civil ordinance against card playing was issued in Paris.

1377, May 23rd – By a vote of 98 to 25, the city council of Florence, Italy forbade the playing of a new card game called 'naibbe.' This was done three years before playing cards were actually introduced into Florence.

1377 – Basle, Switzerland: A monk named Johannes von Rheinfelden wrote, "Thus it is that a certain game, called the game of cards, has reached us in the present year, namely A.D. 1377." He describes a deck with 52 cards, four suits with cards numbered one through ten and court cards consisting of two Marshals and a King. The suits are then described as "some of these signs being considered good but others signifying evil."

1379, May 14 – The account books of Johanna, Duchess of Brabant, and her husband, Wencelsaus of Luxemberg, contain the entry: "Given to Monsieur and Madame four peters, two forms, value eight and a half moutons, wherewith to buy a pack of cards"

1380 – Playing cards were mentioned in the archives of Nuremberg, Germany.

1392 – The earliest known playing cards to have physically survived to the present day are preserved in the *Bibliotheque Nationale* in Paris.

1392 – The French Royal Minister paid one Jacquemin Gringonneur, painter, for three games of cards "in gold and diverse colors, ornamented with many deuces, for the diversion of our Lord, the King." This was the first documented presence of playing cards in Europe.

Late 1300s – The ancestors of the modern cards we use today arrived in Europe from the Mamelukes Dynasty of Egypt. The deck consisted of 52 cards with four suits: polo sticks, coins, swords and cups.

1423 – Date of the earliest known deck of wood-engraved playing cards.

1430s – Meister Ingold, of Alsace, France wrote a treatise called *The Golden Game*, which was one of the first known books about card games.

1439 – German playing cards were 7" x 4" with the suits being hunting dogs, stags, ducks and falcons. The portraits on the cards were almost always painted by women.

1440 – The first known mention of the court cards—Kings, Queens and Knaves—occurred in France.

THE EARLIEST BETTING-BLUFFING TYPE CARD GAMES

1441 – The first known mention of the game of Poch, later Pochen, occurred in Strasburg, Germany.

1450 – The suits of German playing cards were Hearts, Leaves, Bells and Acorns.

1450 – The suits of Swiss playing cards were Shields, Flowers, Bells and Acorns.

1450 – The first known mention of the game Pochspiel occurred in Germany. It's the first known card game to incorporate the elements of betting, hand rankings and bluffing.

1450s – The first known Spanish Playing cards were 1 7/8th inches by 1 5/8th inches. They were very small and nearly square.

1459 – First known reference to card playing occurred in England, from a private letter.

1460 – The spades on French playing cards were stenciled black spikes or spearheads.

1461 – England's King Edward IV's first parliament (Nov. 1461-May 1462) prohibits card playing (and dicing) except for the 12 days of Christmas.

1480 – The first appearance of spades, hearts, clubs and diamonds all together in one deck occurred in France.

1500s – The first 52-card deck of cards appeared in Rouen, France and quickly became known as "the French deck."

1480 – The four Kings in the French decks represented:

K♥ - Charlemagne
K♦ - Julius Caesar
K♣ - Alexander the Great
K♠ - King David, from the Bible

These images have survived and are still in use today because they're drawings that can easily be made from stencils, and therefore, easily produced in large quantities. Competing suits made by rival card makers of the time were made from woodcuts, which were extremely labor intensive to make.

1490s – The lowest card in the deck, the ace, began to be used as the highest card in the deck. This was to symbolize the rise of the lower class. The use of the Ace as the highest card was sporadic until the time of the French Revolution in the late 1700s, after which is became popular and permanent.

1492 – Fearful of horrendous storms, the sailors under the command of Christopher Columbus threw their playing cards overboard. Once on dry land, they regretted their decision and fashioned new cards by drawing images on wide tree leaves.

1500s – Games called "Primera" in Spain and "Primero" in England were popular. There were rounds of betting and the recognized ranks of hands were three-of-a-kind, pairs and a *flux* (flush), which was a three-card flush.

Primero is a game where a player gets two cards followed by a round of betting. Then each player gets two more cards followed by another round of betting. Players then announce what hand they're representing, followed by a final round of betting. The best possible hand is four 7s.

1520 – *The Book on Games of Chance,* by Italian Gerolama Cardona was published. It is the first known book devoted to all of the card games of its time.

> *There are such persons who are constantly pursued*
> *by bad luck. To such I say*—never play.
>
> Gerolama Cardona, 1520

1564 – The first known professional advice regarding card playing was written by Gerolama Cardona when he said,

> *The greatest advantage lies in not playing at all.*

1564 – Gerolama Cardona said, "There is a difference from play with dice, because the latter is open, whereas play with cards takes place from ambush, because they are concealed."

1590 – Date of the oldest known surviving deck of English playing cards.

1600 to 1650 – 500,000 decks of playing cards were sold in England.

1600s – The abbreviation for King (K) and Knave (Kn) in the English deck were so similar that the name of the Knave was changed to Jack.

1600s—WILLIAM SHAKESPEARE ON POKER. Shakespeare mentions cards and card games many times in his various plays. In doing so, he was actually talking about the popular bluffing and betting games of the times—brag and pochen—the forerunners of modern-day poker.

> *Beware of entrance into a jack-pot, but being in, heart that the opposed may beware of thee.*—Hamlet
>
> *Now might I do it pat.*—Hamlet

I cannot draw.—King Lear, v. 3.

This business will raise us all.—Winter's Tale, iv. 4.

I would give all my fame for a pot.—Henry V, iii. 2.

Let him pass peacefully.—Henry VI, 3.

You apprehend passing shrewdly.—Much Ado ii. 1.

I can draw as soon as any other man.—Romeo and Juliet, 1.

It is the curse of Kings.—King John vi. a. (Said King John after making three-of-a-kind and losing to a flush.)

Though setter up and plucker down of kings!—Henry VI. 2.

I have a bobtail.—King Lear, iii. 6.

These begging Jacks.—Merchant of Venice, iii. 4.

We see these things effected to the full.—Henry VI, 1. 2.

Straight let us seek.—King John, v. 7.

1610 – First known use of the word 'deck' to describe what was then universally known as a pack of cards was made by William Shakespeare.

1628, October 22nd – King Charles 1st of England granted a charter providing for royal protection to a company called "The Master, Wardens and Commonality of the Mistery of Playing Cards of the City of London." The purpose was to unify the hundreds of different card makers into a loose union to consolidate card making efforts and to prevent duplication of similar-looking cards. To help them further, the importation of playing cards was forbidden while a duty on playing cards was imposed.

1633 – A Plymouth Colony record reveals that two persons were fined two pounds each for card playing. The penalty for a second offense was to "bee publickly whipt."

As much is lost by a card too many as a card too few.

Miguel Cervantes
Don Quixote, 1635

1665 – First known use of the English word 'bluff' as it applies to modern-day poker.

*So intermix your care with joy, you may
Lighten you labour by a little joy.*

Charles Cotton, 1674
The Compleate Gamester

*He speaks the language of the game he plays at,
better than the language of his country.*

Charles Cotton, 1674
The Compleate Gamester

1685 – The French Governor of Canada, Jacques de Meulles, used playing cards as legal tender currency when he paid off war debts with them.

1700s – A five-card game called Brag incorporating betting and bluffing was played in England, as Pochen in Germany and as Poque in France. It was the French game of Poque that is played in the French possession of Louisiana that was later mispronounced as 'poker' by the Americans.

1703 – Card playing was banned in Boston.

1720 – Playing cards were sold in New York and Boston for one shilling per pack.

1725 – The English game of Brag was mentioned by Charles Cotton in *The Compleat Gamester*:

> The nature of it is, that you are to endeavor to impose upon the judgment of the rest that play, and particularly upon the person that chiefly offers to oppose you, by boasting of cards in your hand, whether Pair Royals, Pairs, or others, that you are better than his or hers that play against you....

1732 – Philadelphia printer Benjamin Franklin advertised the sale of playing cards in his first *Poor Richard's Almanach*.

1735, October – "A child of James and Elizabeth Leesh of Chester le Street, was played at for cards, at the sign of the Salmon, one game, four shillings against the child, by Henry and John Trotter, Robert Thomson and Thomas Ellison, which was won by the latter, and delivered to them accordingly."

Local Records & C., of Remarkable Events
Compiled by John Sykes, 1824

1742 – Edmond Hoyle's book *A Short Treatise on the Game of Whist* was published. Actually, the complete title of his book was *A Short Treatise on the Game of Whist, containing the laws of the game; and also some Rules whereby a Beginner may, with due attention to them, attain to the Playing it well....* Incredibly, the book does not say a word about how to play the game of Whist!

1745 – Benjamin Franklin used cutouts of playing cards to aid in his experiments with electricity.

1750 – The Queen replaced the Knave as a court card in England.

1751 – Edmond Hoyle published *A Short Treatise on the Game of Brag*. The book also covers the card games of piquet and quadrille. Only two copies are known to have survived to present day.

1765 – Playing cards were used as passes to admit students to their classes at the University of Pennsylvania.

1765, November 1st – The infamous Stamp Act levied a tax of one shilling on each pack of playing cards.

1766, March 17th – The Stamp Act was repealed, having been law for only 136 days.

Kings themselves have been known to play off, at Primero,
not only all the money and jewels they could part with,
but with the very images of the churches.

Oliver Goldsmith, 1767

1769, August 29th – Edmond Hoyle died in London at either age 90 or 97, depending on whom you believe. Other than his books on Whist and Brag, little was known about him except that he once described himself as a 'gentlemen' and he was rumored to have been a barrister, or lawyer.

1770, September 5th – George Washington's diary entry read, "At home all day playing cards."

1777, May 8th – General George Washington issued the following order to his army:

"….the Commander-in-Chief in the most pointed and explicit terms forbids ALL officers and soldiers playing at cards, dice or any games except those of EXERCISE for diversion; being impossible if the practice be allowed at to discriminate between innocent play for amusement and criminal gaming for pecuniary and sordid purposes."

1790s – The lack of an index (numbers in the corners) and the fact that court cards had full-length figures meant that playing cards had to be spread out with both hands for a player to know exactly what his cards were.

1795 – Card playing was introduced to North American Indians by Spanish conquistadors.

1801 – The first known instance in which the numbers of the cards appeared in the upper right-hand corner occurred in Spanish-made cards.

THE ORIGINS OF AMERICAN-STYLE POKER

1803, July 4th—There is no one exact, single day when American-style poker was invented. However, this author nominates July 4th, 1803 as the adopted date of the creation of poker. It's the day that President Thomas Jefferson announced the Louisiana Purchase to the nation. Since an early version of poker was being played in the predominately French city of New Orleans, and this event opened up the territory for expansion, it created the conditions necessary for the rapid evolution of the modern game of poker.

1810s – A trader at the San Carlos Indian Reservation in Arizona discovered a pack of American playing cards made from what is believed to be the skins of white men.

1812 – The first steamboat to operate on the Mississippi River is Robert Fulton's *New Orleans.*

1814 – The United States Treasury reported that 400,000 packs of playing cards were manufactured that year with a duty of 25 cents per pack.

1815 – The city of New Orleans, Louisiana licensed casino-style gambling.

1820s – American Indians gambled profusely, betting all of their worldly possessions, their horses, tee pees and wives centuries before white men introduced them to gambling. Wives lost to gambling often nonchalantly took up residence with the winner, knowing that they would soon be lost back to their original husbands.

1820 – There were exactly twenty gambling steamboats operating on the Mississippi River.

1820 – Accounts of a game called 'Whiskey Poker' were found. It is the ancestor of all modern poker games played in North America today, although the original game is no longer played.

1823 – The state of Louisiana legalized most forms of gambling, including the game of Poque.

In play there are two pleasures for your choosing—
the one is winning, and the other losing.

George Gordon, Lord Byron
Don Juan, 1826

1824 – The Austrian card company Piatnik was founded. They are still a very successful, thriving producer of playing cards to this day.

1827 – John Davis, an émigré from Saint Dominique, opened a multi-building luxury casino called The Crescent City House in New Orleans on Orleans Street between Bourbon and Royal Streets. It had the first known legal poker room in history. The casino was open 24/7 and patrons were provided with free rooms, drinks and meals. Obviously, this casino was used as a model for the casinos opened 120 years later in Las Vegas.

1827 – Double-headed court cards were first used in France.

1828 – Up to this time, England charged a tax of one-half crown on each deck of cards. Once the tax was paid, the proof of payment was stamped on the A♠ and only then could it legally be included in the deck. This practice eventually led to card makers also using the A♠ to imprint their company name, logo and other information.

1829 – The poker deck of this time consisted of only twenty cards—four each of Aces, Kings, Queens, Jacks and Tens. The best possible hand was either four aces or four kings, if you had four kings and one of the aces. There was no draw and the only recognized hands were pairs, trips and 4-of-a-kind. Straights and flushes were not recognized.

1829 – A book entitled *Exposure of the Arts and Miseries of Gambling,* written by Jonathan H. Green in 1834 but not published until 1843 contains the description of the first known poker game played in the United States, played in 1829.

1829, August 1ˢᵗ – George Devol was born in Marietta, Ohio. He left home at the age of ten to become a riverboat cabin boy. There he learned how to play poker, faro and three-card Monte. He became a professional cheat at all of these games by the age of seventeen. He then stole thousands of dollars from travelers and gamblers who rode on his riverboat on the Ohio and Mississippi Rivers. He could false-shuffle, false-cut, stack a deck, deal from the bottom of the deck or run up a hand as well as any professional many years his senior.

George Devol followed the U.S. Army during the Mexican War, winning—or more correctly—stealing thousands of dollars from paymasters and soldiers alike. He stole from every person he ever came in contact with and he never played an honest game of anything in his life. However, there's a legitimate reason he's an important figure in the history of poker.

Before he died in Hot Springs, Arkansas (boyhood home of President Bill Clinton) in 1903, he wrote a book about his exploits as a professional card sharp and traveler entitled *40 Years A Gambler on the Mississippi*. It is not an instructional guide or rulebook on how to play poker. Rather, it's a well-written, entertaining, historical account of what life was like for riverboat gamblers. It contains 180 short stories describing his successes and bad beats. The book is so remarkably entertaining that it's still in print even though its copyright expired years ago.

1829, December – The first account of poker being played in America was written about by English actor Joseph Cowell. He observed a game while traveling from Louisville to New Orleans on the steamboat *Helen M'Gregor*. One of the players was Speaker of House Henry Clay.

1830 – Poker players could buy a pack of marked cards advertised in newspapers and catalogues from the E.N. Grandine Co. of New York for $1.25 per pack or $10 for a dozen. These cards were shipped by mail and express pony to card players all over North America.

1831 – Abraham Lincoln played penny-ante poker while piloting a flatboat from Illinois to New Orleans.

1832 – Edward Pendleton opened The Palace of Fortune, a casino with private rooms for playing poker. Daniel Webster and Henry Clay played against each other regularly. Most pots were well over $1,000.

Cards are war, in disguise of a sport.

Charles Lamb
Essays of Elia, 1832

1833 – Modern-day use of spades, clubs hearts and diamonds in North America comes from the French.

1833 – The fifty-two card deck is first used in America. During the twenty years that it took to gain nationwide popular acceptance, the extra cards in the deck (52 vs. 20) allowed for the creation of many more poker games and for several more players to play in each game.

1834 – Jonathan H. Green describes poker and calls it "the cheating game" in his book *An Exposure of the Arts and Miseries of Gambling*.

1835- Louisiana repeals all of its laws allowing gambling. Casino gambling was declared illegal.

1836 – American-style poker was mentioned in "*Dragoon Campaigns to the Rocky Mountains,*" by James Hildreth. On pages 128-130 he describes a late-night game in the soldiers' barracks, "The M-{ajor} lost some cool hundreds last night at poker…."

1837, May 27 – James Butler "Wild Bill" Hickok was born in Troy Grove, Illinois.

Late 1830s – Fifty-two card decks were popular on the Mississippi River gambling steamboats but not yet on the East Coast.

1840 – Date of the first known 5-card draw poker game. It was known as "Draw Poke."

1840s – What we call 'stacking the deck' today was originally known as 'stock the deck.'

1843 – Jonathan Harrington Green's book, *Exposure of the Arts and Miseries of Gambling*, was published. Actually, the full title was "*An Exposure of the Arts and Miseries of Gambling, Designed Especially as a Warning to the Youthful and Inexperienced Against the Evils of That Odious and Destructive Vice.*" Later in the year it was republished with the new title *Gamblers Exposed*.

1845 – *American Hoyle* mentions a game called "Twenty-Card Poker" and another game called "Poker or Bluff." It also mentioned a game called "Poke."

1845 – There were 557 gambling steamboats operating on the Mississippi River.

1846 – His Honor, Walter Cotton, the Mayor of Monterey, California issued one of the first known ordinances against gambling in North America: "A vice which shows itself here more on the Sabbath than any other day of the week."

1846 – Ulysses S. Grant played brag between battles during the Mexican War.

1847 – U.S. gamblers, and card players, in particular, followed the conquering U.S. Army into Mexico City during the Mexican war. After discovering that the Mexicans were scrupulously honest card players and knew nothing of cheating, they ordered 14,400 decks of marked playing cards from a New York supplier to introduce into Mexico City.

1848 – The San Francisco Town Council passed an ordinance against gambling and card playing; however, they quickly repealed it because they needed the tax revenue card playing generated.

Mid-1800s – The first true Joker was added to the deck to act as the "Best Bower" in the game of Euchre, as it still is today. Poker players borrowed it, using it as any card they choose to help improve their hands. The joker does not come from the fool in tarot cards as is popularly believed.

Mid 1800s – Apache Indians created their own decks of cards by painting images on deerskin and hides. Their decks consisted of forty cards with ten cards in each of four suits. The ten cards were, 2, 3, 4, 5, 6, 7, the page (equal to a jack) knight, king and ace.

1850 – A playing card manufacturer from New York featured portraits of George and Martha Washington on the ace of spades.

1850 – With the fifty-two card deck having been in use for about fifteen years or more, 7-Card Stud is now a popular poker game of choice.

1850 – The *English Hoyle* (also known as *Bohn's Handbook of Games*) does not mention poker but its American reprint does mention poker in its addendum. This is the first-ever mention of poker in any rulebook.

1850 – San Francisco gambling houses purposefully employed female dealers because they believed that outright cheating by a female dealer was more likely to be overlooked or forgiven by the male clientele.

I cheat my boys every chance I get.
I want to make 'em sharp.

William Rockefeller, 1850
(John D.'s father)

1850-1890 – Riverboat card players bought their cards from the ship's bartenders. Even though the decks were new and still in their original unopened packaging, with their unbroken seals, they were still marked. The bartenders were paid well by the cheating poker players to keep them in stock.

1850 – The draw, as in 5-Card Draw, was first mentioned in a handbook of games.

1850 – *Hoyle's Games* for the first time describes a 52 card deck, a stud game with ten players and no draw, and a bonus for making trips or better.

1850 – Unscrupulous printers began creating look-alike, but marked- decks of cards of the most popular brands.

1850s – A typical steamboat operating on the Mississippi River was 140 feet long, 28 feet wide, could carry as much as 200 tons (400,000 lbs) of cargo and up to fifty passengers. It could go 10 mph down the river and 4 mph up the river.

1850s – Children as young as ten and twelve years old frequented California gambling house card rooms, losing hundreds of dollars a day.

1850s – San Francisco had more than 1,000 gambling houses where poker could be played.

1850 – This is the probable first year that 5-Card Stud was played. The game originated in the Ohio-Indiana-Illinois area.

1851 – Double-headed court cards were first used in England.

1851 – One California lumber company paid its worker with vouchers that could be redeemed at local gambling houses, instead of paying them in cash.

1851, February 17th – Alice Ivers was born in Sudbury, England. She was the first known professional female full-time poker player in the world. By the end of her life, she was known as Poker Alice. When she was in her early 20's she moved to Colorado and married Frank Duffield. Very soon after that he was killed in a dynamite/mining accident, but not before he taught his wife how to play poker, count cards, figure pot odds and how to bluff.

She then made her way through all of the Colorado gambling hot spots of the time—Alamosa, Georgetown, Trinidad, Central City, Leadville and Silver City, New Mexico before finally moving to South Dakota. She married Warren G. Tubbs in Deadwood and had seven children with him, all the while maintaining her 'job' as a full-time poker player. She was so good that she could often win as much as $6,000 in one night of poker playing.

When her husband died of pneumonia in the winter of 1910 she buried him and then went straight to a poker game. Over the next twenty years she owned and operated a bordello, became a bootlegger, accidentally killed a U.S. Army soldier, took up smoking cigars and did time in prison for multiple convictions for operating a house of ill-repute. At the age of 75, she was pardoned by the governor.

Poker Alice estimated that she won more than $250,000 by gambling and playing poker in her lifetime and more importantly, she *never* cheated. Since she was a celebrity of sorts, her life and times were well documented. Because of that, contemporary accounts of her activities and historical researchers all agree that she was telling the truth.

1851, August 14th—The baptismal docket of the Presbyterian Church in the town of Griffin, in Spalding County, Georgia shows that John Henry "Doc" Holliday was born that day. A birth certificate did exist but was burned during Sherman's march through Georgia during the Civil War.

John Henry Holliday was born into a wealthy, genteel, high-class family shortly before the beginning of the Civil War. After the war, he went to Philadelphia, Pennsylvania to attend dental school. There he earned a genuine, bona-fide, medical degree and a license to practice dentistry. Many poker players have gone by the name of "Doc" (including this author) in the past century and a half, but Doc Holliday was the first to actually be a doctor.

Shortly after returning to Georgia with his medical degree, he was diagnosed with tuberculosis. He then decided to move his dental practice to Dallas, Texas where he could take advantage of the warm, dry weather. He quickly discovered that his constant coughing scared off his customers but he didn't mind because he preferred to spend his time in saloons and card rooms. He used the thick, smoke-filled air as a cover for his constant coughing. In no time at all, he killed a popular city leader in a dispute over a $500 pot in a poker game.

Later that night he abruptly, but cheerfully, moved to Jacksborough, Texas. While there, he killed a U.S. Union Army soldier during a poker game. He then moved to Denver, Colorado, where he nearly killed a poker player over a disputed pot. The player lost three fingers and one eye and barely survived. He then moved to Fort Griffin where killed a fellow poker player over a $50 pot in a 5-card stud game.

He was arrested, thrown in jail and escaped when the jail caught fire. He then fled to Trinidad, Colorado where he shot and left for dead another poker player. He then went to Las Vegas, New Mexico where he killed yet another poker player. He then fled to Dodge City, Kansas. While there, he was persuaded by Wyatt Earp to move to the dry, hot town of Tombstone, Arizona. While passing through Santa Fe, New Mexico on his was to Tombstone, he killed three more of his fellow poker players who thought he was a bit too lucky.

Shortly after arriving in Tombstone he killed one Bud Philpot and this time it had nothing to do with poker. It was because he was spreading gossip about him. He then participated in the famous shootout at the O.K. Corral and in the subsequent trial for that, he was found not guilty by reason of self-defense.

Now in the later stages of his disease and continuously coughing up blood, he rode the 800 miles back to Colorado on horseback—*alone*. The state of Arizona tried to have him extradited to stand trial for the murder of another poker player. The Governor of Colorado protected him by refusing to sign the extradition papers and Doc Holliday died in bed in Glenwood Springs, Colorado on November 8th, 1887, at age only 36.

The exact location of his grave is unknown. His grave site was moved to allow for highway construction and the records that would reveal where he's now buried have been lost.

1855 – Novelist George Eliot (Mary Anne Evans) diary entry read: "One night we attempted "Brag" or "Pocher.""

1857 – *Hoyle's Games*, published in New York City, said, "….20-card poker is one of the most dangerous pitfalls to be found in the city."

1860 – There were 735 gambling steamboats operating on the Mississippi River.

1860, May 18th – Republicans nominated Abraham Lincoln for President and Hannibal Hamlin as his running mate for Vice President. Hamlin was in his Washington D.C. hotel room playing poker when a crowd burst in to tell him the good news. His dry reply was, "You people have ruined a good hand."

1860s – A deck of cards was referred to as "The Devil's Picture Gallery" by preachers and anti-gambling proponents.

1860s – The joker was more commonly called a 'cuter' or 'imperial trump' that could be used as an ace.

1861 to 1865 – Civil War soldiers on both sides played poker but threw their cards away before a battle because they considered them to be "instruments of the Devil" and believed it was a curse to be killed in battle while carrying them.

1862 – Confederate soldiers played a poker game called Mistigris. It's the French word for joker and the joker was wild.

1862 – The first known playing cards to be manufactured in Mexico were made this year.

1863 – A Union Army paymaster was taken prisoner by a small band of Confederate soldiers, along with his $50,000 payroll. Almost immediately, a poker game broke out with the Confederate soldiers allowing their paymaster prisoner to play in the game. By nightfall the paymaster had all the money and before they could decide what to do with him, he was rescued by Union soldiers.

1864 – *American Hoyle* gives the ranks of poker hands as: one pair, two pairs, straight sequence or rotation, triplets, flush, full-house, and fours. Then add, "When a straight and a flush come together, it outranks a full."

1864 – The straight was first recognized as a legitimate poker hand. This included 'around the corner straights' such as Q♠ K♣ A♥ 2♦ 3♠.

1864 – *Hoyle's Games* stated:

> "Success in playing the game of Poker (or Bluff, as it is sometimes called) depends rather upon luck and energy than skill. It is emphatically a game of chance, and there are easier ways of cheating, or playing with marked cards, than in any other game".

1864, October 31st – Nevada was admitted to the Union with a state constitution that permitted gambling.

1865 – Confederate General Nathan Bedford Forrest turned his last $10 into $1,500 in one night of poker playing, against his wife's strong urging that he not go to the game.

1867 – *Hoyle's Games* mentions for the first time that a straight, a flush and an ante had been added to the game of poker. It also mentions for the first time in print the game of draw poker.

1867 – *Hoyle's Games* mentions 7-Card Stud for the first time. Seven-card stud was created as a solution to some of the problems with 5-Card stud. In 5-Card Stud, all of the betting centers around the unknown value of your opponents' single down card. The problem was that it was too easy for cheaters to know what that card was. So, a new game was created that gave each player two down cards and a third down card at the end.

1867 to 1890 – 7-Card Stud was more popularly known as "5-Card Stud with two extra cards."

1869 – Shoshone Indian women were voracious card players, often betting and losing their husbands' possessions.

1870 – Double-headed court cards are first seen in America.

1870 – First known mention of a poker game called Jackpots occurred in Toledo, Ohio. The game called for the first player to bet at the pot (the opener) to be holding at least a pair of Jacks or better. The purpose of the required openers was to cut down on the wild and crazy betting and bluffing with nothing.

Remember that Fortune does not like people to be overjoyed at her favours, and that she prepares bitter deceptions for the imprudent, who are intoxicated by success.

Andrew Steinmetz,
The Gaming Table, 1870

1870s – Bluffing was known as the 'art of coffee-house.'

1870s – The wild cards in poker came about as a way to make use of the blank card or two that traditionally came with every deck.

1872 – American-style poker was introduced to England by the American – Ambassador to the Court of St. James (England) Major General Robert C. Schenk.

1873 – General Schenck wrote a 4-page pamphlet titled *A Flowery Path to Wealth: The Game of Draw Poker as Taught to the English Aristocracy.* It was the first book of rules for American-style draw poker. Poker in England quickly became known as "Schenck Poker".

1872, December 9th – Pinckney Pinchback became Governor of Louisiana. He was George Devol's black servant and cheating partner. He made so much money cheating at cards that he was able to finance his political campaigns with it. He was the first non-white and first person of African American descent to become Governor of a state.

1872 – California outlawed "stud horse poker." It was a house game with a built-in percentage for the house.

At the gaming-table all men are equal; no superiority, birth, accomplishments, or ability avail here; great noble men, merchants, orators, jockeys, statesmen, and idlers here thrown together.

Charles Greville
Memoirs, 1874

1875 – One *New York Times* writer wrote:

"....forced to the conclusion that the national pastime is not base-ball, but poker."

1875 – *Hoyle's Games* mentions jackpot poker and the use of a joker as a wild card.

1875 – Well-known, popular and highly-skilled American Indian poker player White Geese Sounding on Waters—better known as Poker Jim—issued sage poker advice: "Two pair not much good."

> *There are few things that are so unpardonably neglected*
> *in our country as poker. The upper class knows very little*
> *about it. Now and then you find ambassadors who have sort*
> *of a general knowledge of the game, but the ignorance of the*
> *people is fearful. Why, I have known clergymen, good men,*
> *kind-hearted, liberal, sincere, and all that, who did not know*
> *the meaning of a "flush." It is enough to make one ashamed*
> *of the species.*
>
> Mark Twain, 1875

1876 – The first time that playing cards were made with rounded instead of square corners. They were called Squeezers because players could fan them out to easily read the indices.

1876, August 2nd – James Butler "Wild Bill" Hickok, was shot and killed by Jack "Crooked Nose" McCall in the Mann-Lewis Saloon in Deadwood, South Dakota. He was 39 years old. At precisely 4:10 p.m. Wild Bill Hickok was playing five-card draw at a poker table with Carl Mann, Charles Rich and Captain Massey, who was a retired riverboat captain. He was sitting with his back to the door instead of in his usual seat on the opposite side of the table with his back to the wall.

Just as he discarded three cards in his hand and as his replacement cards were being dealt to him, Jack McCall nonchalantly walked up behind him. Just as Hickok picked up his second card and as his third card was sliding across the table to him from the dealer, a bullet from an 1851 .36 Colt pistol entered the back of his head and exited from his right cheek. The bullet then went on to enter Captain Massey's right arm.

Cards went flying. Cash, chips, cigars, tables and people hit the floor in every direction at once. Jack McCall left the saloon and took a seat at a bar down the street. He was quickly apprehended. He later said that he didn't try to make a run for it because he honestly thought he had done the town a favor and he would be congratulated for it. Doc Pierce, the town's undertaker was summoned. When he arrived he found Hickok dead on the floor lying in the fetal position with four cards lying beside him—A♠ A♣ 8♠ 8♣.

Little known is the fact that McCall's gun (it was a .36 caliber and not a .45 caliber as is almost always erroneously reported) was later tested and it was discovered that even though there were bullets in all six chambers, the only bullet that would fire was the one that killed Hickok. All five of the other bullets misfired.

McCall killed Hickok because he thought he had been cheated out of a twenty-five cent pot. This was probably true because Hickok was a terrible poker player, he usually cheated when he did play and he was very blatant and open about it. No one ever made an issue of it because he had a habit or drawing his guns to end the conversation on that subject.

McCall was found guilty of murder in a speedy trial by the local citizenry and hanged on March 1st, 1877. President Ulysses S. Grant personally refused to commute his sentence to life in prison. He was buried with the hangman's noose still tightly wrapped around his neck.

It has been variously reported through the years that Hickok's fifth card was either the Q♠, the J♦, the 9♦ or the Q♥, but these guesses are all wrong. There never was a fifth card because a bullet went through his head the moment he picked up his fourth card and before his fifth card reached him. This fact is incontrovertibly corroborated by Captain Massey and Harry Young, the bartender who witnessed the action. The poker hand found by his body—Aces and 8s—has since become known as "The Dead Man's Hand." Wild Bill Hickok was inducted into the Poker Hall of Fame in 1979.

1877 – William "Canada Bill" Jones died in Reading, Pennsylvania, age unknown.

A pair of six-shooters beats a pair of sixes.

Belle Starr, 1877

1878—House rules posted in a poker room in a saloon in Leadville, Colorado:

A club member must be a gentleman.
A gentleman plays according to the rules:
1. Watch your language.
2. Pass, call, check and bet in turn.
3. Show one—show all.
4. Do not show your cards until play is completed.
5. All checked and called hands must be placed on the table—FIVE CARDS faced up.
6. No talking about the hand or the plays if you are out of the pot (until play is completed).
7. No rabbit hunting.
8. Announce all raises and the amount of the raise.
9. Dealers must not look at top cards—at any time.
10. No sharking.
11. No string bets.
12. No automatic insurance.
13. In stud poker the dealer must deal the first card face down.
14. No looking at the deadwood at any time.

1879 – Mark Twain's favorite poker game was 5-Card Draw.

1880s – Professional riverboat card players resorted to dressing as common farmers, businessmen, cross-country travelers or even clergymen due to their well-earned unsavory reputations.

1880s – Origin of the word 'nuts' to describe the best possible poker hand. Poker players out West could bet their horse and wagon rig but obviously couldn't put them on the poker table when the bet was made. They also didn't have a deed or title to show ownership. So they would take the nuts off the wheels and put them in the pot. This made it difficult for them to make a quick exit if they lost the hand, as the wheels would easily come off the wagon. This meant that a player who bet the nuts usually had the best hand.

1880 to 1939 – Most of the popular poker chips used during this period were made of a clay composition.

1880 – 5-Card Stud became known as 'short stud' to differentiate it from the increasingly popular new game of 7-Card Stud.

Put not your trust in Kings and Princes:
Three of a kind will take them both.

Robert C. Schenk, 1880
Rules For Playing Poker

1880s – Indexed playing cards finally became the norm although unindexed cards were still in use and could easily be found.

1881, June 28th – The Russell, Morgan and Co., which later became the U.S. Playing Card Company, printed their first deck of cards. Twenty employees made 1600 decks of cards that day.

Money has no value except to back a good hand.

Jefferson Randolph "Soapy Smith
1882

1885 – Most of the wild, fast and loose poker games in the East evaporated as most card players favored going west to California to take advantage of the gold miners.

1887 – The joker first appeared in decks of Canadian cards made by the Union Card and Paper Company of Montreal.

1887 – George Devol published *Forty Years a Gambler on the Mississippi.*

1887 – Rider Back (Bicycle) playing cards were manufactured by the Russell, Morgan and Company for the first time. The design was the idea submitted in a contest by employee 'Gus' Berens, who won a prize for his idea.

1887, November 8th – John Henry "Doc" Holliday died of tuberculosis in Glenwood Springs, Colorado. He was 36 years old. Having lived the life that he did, he always expected that he would die with his boots on. When he realized that he was about to die in bed with his boots off, his last words were, "Well I'll be damned. This is funny."

1888 – Instructions for using a holdout machine, according to the Ohio Historical Society:

1. Practice at least three weeks a month with the machine, to get it down fine.
2. Don't work the machine too much. Three or four times a night are enough.
3. Never play it in a small (low limit) game.
4. Holding out one card will beat any square game in the world.
5. Holding out two cards can be very strong but can't easily be played on smart people.
6. Three cards are too many to hold out on smart men, as a 'full' (house) is too big (a hand) to be held without acting as an eye-opener.
7. Never, under any circumstances, hold out four or five cards.
8. One card is enough, as you are really playing with six cards to everyone else's five.
9. If you are an expert, you can play the machine on your own deal; but it looks better if you do it on someone else's.

1889, April 13th – Herbert O. Yardley was born in Worthington, Indiana.

1890s – Apache war chief Geronimo, while interred at Fort Sill, Oklahoma, spent his days enthusiastically playing poker.

1890s – A magazine called *Poker Chips* was published. It was the first known magazine devoted entirely to the game of poker.

> *One should always play fair when one has the winning cards.*
>
> Oscar Wilde, 1890

1891 – Poker card machines were invented. There were more than 3,000 of them placed in Brooklyn licensed liquor establishments.

1891 – Section 330 of the California Penal Code banned poker.

1891 – The Broadmoor Casino opened in Colorado City, Colorado, which became part of Colorado Springs in 1917. The casino drew more than 15,000 gamblers and poker players every day.

> *When I told Canada Bill the game he was playing*
> *in was crooked, he said, "I know it is, but it's the*
> *only game in town."*

George Devol, 1892
Forty Years a Gambler on the Mississippi

1893 – Nicholas Andrea "Nick the Greek" Dandalos was born in Rethymnon, Greece.

A priest rebuked a gambler for the time he wasted
at play. "Yes," replied the latter, "there is a lot of
time lost in shuffling the cards."

Charles Heckethorn, 1898
The Gambling World

Whiskey has pushed more money across the table
to sober men than all the dumb players on earth.

John Dunn, 1897

1895—The first known poker book to be written by a woman, *Poker—The Modern Game, with Passing Description of Its Origin* (LOC# GV1251.C15), was written by Alice Howard Cady.

1900 – Probable first time that Texas Hold'em was played. It comes from the Robstown, Texas (Corpus Christi) area and was originally known as Hold'em or Hold Me Darling.

1900 – Date of the first known game of split pot, or high-low poker.

1900 – Cassius Marcellus Coolidge contracted with the advertising firm Brown & Bigelow of St. Paul, Minnesota, to paint a series of sixteen oil paintings of dogs in various human poses. Nine of the sixteen became "Dogs Playing Poker."

1901 – Only thirty people lived in Las Vegas.

1901 – Pat Garrett, when applying for the job of Customs Collector of El Paso, Texas, was personally interviewed for the job by President Teddy Roosevelt. In order to get the job, Garrett had to explicitly promise to not play poker while in office. He got the job.

1900 to 1932 – U.S. Congressman John Nance Garner, a Texan and Vice-President beginning in 1933, made more money from playing poker than he did from his salary as a U.S. Congressman.

1901 – Poker card machines in Brooklyn were redesigned to allow the play of draw poker.

1902—After playing poker for more than thirty years in all of the popular Western gambling towns, Bat Masterson moved to New York City to take up permanent residence. Within a week, he was arrested for playing in an illegal poker game.

1903 – The acceptance of high-low split poker led to the idea of playing poker for low only. This, in turn, led to the creation of Lowball.

1904, November 20th – Benny Binion was born in Grayson County, Texas.

> POKER, n. *A game said to be played with cards for some purpose to this lexicographer unknown.*
>
> Ambrose Bierce, 1906
> *The Devil's Dictionary*

1907, April 1st – The Arizona and New Mexico Territorial Governments prohibited all forms of gambling. This was done to increase their chances of being admitted to the Union as states. *Century Magazine* reported that one of the former Phoenix poker players complained, "The place is dead now. Every man, woman and beast goes to bed at eight o'clock. Sleeping has become one of our principal industries." Both territories became states in 1912.

1907, May 14th – Johnny Moss was born in Marshall, Texas.

1910 – Nevada closed all of its casinos.

1911 – In California, legislation prohibited stud poker as a game of luck. The law held that draw poker, however, was legal because it was a game of skill. California Attorney General Harold Sigel Webb said draw poker was a "game of science rather than chance."

1911 – A bill was introduced into the Missouri legislature to license poker players in order to prevent "millions of dollars lost annually by incompetent and foolish players who do not know the value of a poker hand."

1912, February 17th—The first known movie to feature poker as its main topic was released. It was an 11-minute silent movie titled *A Cure For Pokeritis*, released by the Vitagraph Company of America and starred John Bunny and Flora Finch. You can watch the movie today on youtube.com.

1915 – U.S. Army West Point Cadet Dwight D. Eisenhower wrote in one of his letters, "....preferring to devote my time to poker." When he graduated later in the year, he was able to buy his first new uniform with his poker winnings.

1918, November—U.S. Army Captain Harry S Truman, while waiting to be shipped back to the States from France after the war ended, played what he called "an almost continuous poker game" for two months.

1919 – *Hoyle's Games* mentions "Deuces Wild" for the first time.

Trust everybody, but cut the cards.

Peter Finley Dunne, 1919

1919 – *Hoyle's Games* describes a community card poker game called Wild Widow. Each player is dealt four cards face down followed by a round of betting. A single community card is turned face up followed by a second round of betting. Players then make their best 5-card hand.

1920s – Prohibition led to the explosion in the number of home games as illegal gambling establishments were closed down.

1920s – Only three poker games are legal in Las Vegas: Stud, Draw and Lowball.

1921 – President Warren Harding told his poker playing buddies, known as his poker cabinet, "Forget that I'm the President of the United States. I'm Warren Harding, playing poker with friends, and I'm going to beat hell out of them." His poker cabinet consisted of Senator Albert Fall, Vice-President Charles Curtis, Speaker of the House Nicholas Longworth, his wife (and Teddy Roosevelt's daughter) Alice Longworth, and other cabinet members.

1921, October 25th – Bartholomew William Barclay "Bat" Masterson died of a heart attack while at work at his *Morning Telegraph* desk. He was 67 years old.

1925 – First documented game of Texas Hold'em played in Dallas, Texas.

> *Almost all gamesters learn to control their faces....*
> *The Hand blabs secrets shamelessly.*
>
> Stephan Zweig, 1926
> *Four-and-Twenty Hours in a Woman's Life*

1928—Gangster Al Capone's favorite place to play poker was in The Oakroom of the Seelbach Hotel in Louisville, Kentucky. The hotel is still operating today and their website advertises: "Today, you can dine in a small alcove in The Oakroom where Capone would play cards."

1928 – John Von Neumann published *On the Theory of Parlor Games*. It was the first scientific and theoretical look at bluffing.

1928, December 31st – 1972 World Series of Poker Champion Thomas Austin "Amarillo Slim" Preston was born.

1929, January 13th – Wyatt Earp died in Los Angeles, California of natural causes at age 81.

1929, January 29th – 1973 World Series of Poker Champion Walter Clyde "Puggy" Pearson was born in Tennessee.

1930, February 27th – Poker Alice Tubbs died in Sturgis, South Dakota of cancer of the gall bladder at age 79.

1930 – U.S. Army officer Dwight D. Eisenhower quits playing poker. As a career military man, he said, "I decided that I had to quit playing. It was not because I didn't enjoy the game—I really love to play. But it had become clear that it was no game to play in the Army." He took up playing poker again after becoming President.

1930, June 16th – 1982 World Series of Poker Champion Jack "Treetop" Straus was born.

1930s – Entertainer, comedian and movie star Groucho Marx got his name because he always carried his poker winnings in a 'grouch bag.' He was a chronic cheat at the game.

1931 – Nevada legalized casino gambling.

1931 – The first legal casino license in Las Vegas was issued to a woman—Maxine Stocker. Her husband worked for the railroad and if the license had been issued in his name they would have fired him for entering the gambling business.

1932 to April, 1945 – President Franklin D. Roosevelt played low limit 7-Card stud (with one-eyed Jacks wild) nearly every evening with friends in his study. His doctor played in the game in order to ensure that the President went to bed by 11pm. His other favorite game was Woolworth's, a poker game where 5s and Tens are wild. (The one-eyed jacks are the J♠ and the J♥.)

1933, August 10th – 1976 and 1977 World Series of Poker Champion Doyle "Texas Dolly" Brunson was born in Longworth, Texas. He got his nickname when, in the early 1970's, Jimmy "The Greek" Snyder mispronounced his name.

1933 to 1941 – During many of President Franklin Roosevelt's radio fireside speeches, his words were often obliterated and made unintelligible by a continuous, annoying, clicking sound. That was him, absent-mindedly playing with and clicking a handful of poker chips that he had brought with him straight from the poker game.

1935 – 1986 World Series of Poker Champion Berry Johnston was born.

Never mix cards and whisky unless
you were weaned on Irish poteen.

Margaret Mitchell, 1936
Gone With the Wind

1937 – A new deck of cards with a new, fifth, suit called Eagle was introduced in America. The purpose was to help stimulate the economy by inducing the public to buy new decks of cards. It was an instant failure.

1937 – Harrah's Casino opened in Reno, Nevada.

1937, December 25th – 1999 World Series of Poker Champion J.J. "Noel" Furlong was born in Dublin, Ireland.

1938 – Herbert O. Yardley said, "Stud poker is not a very difficult game after you see your opponent's hole card."

1938 – The city of Gardena, California legalizes poker. The first card rooms were the Rainbow, Monterey, Gardena, Horseshoe, Normandie and the El Dorado. They rented seats for $1 to $10 per hour, depending on the stakes. There was no professional dealer. Each player had to deal his own hand. Each card room was limited by law to a maximum of 35 tables each.

1938 – The Lord Chief Justice of England declared poker to be illegal, as he said it was a game of chance.

1939 – Las Vegas had 6 casinos and 16 saloons.

1940 – First year plastic poker chips were used.

1941 – The El Rancho Casino was the first casino to open on the Las Vegas strip.

1941 to 1945 – Poker expert John Scarne was hired by the U.S military to tour the world teaching GIs how not to be cheated at cards.

1942, December 29th – 1984 World Series of Poker Champion Jack Keller was born.

1942 to 1945 – The U.S. Playing Card Company made playing cards specifically intended for American prisoners of war held by the Germans during WWII. When moistened or soaked in water, they came apart to reveal maps of possible escape routes.

1942 to 1945 – U.S. Military playing cards depicted:

K♦ - President Franklin D. Roosevelt
K♠ - Prime Minister Winston Churchill
K♣ - General Charles de Gaulle
K♥ - Joseph Stalin
The Joker – Adolph Hitler, with a 500-lb bomb over his head.

1943 to 1945 – U.S. Navy Lieutenant Commander Richard M. "Nick" Nixon won more than $6,000 playing poker while assigned as a supply officer in the South Pacific during WWII. He used that money to finance a campaign for the U.S. House of Representatives in 1946, which he won.

1944, November 14th – 1983 World Series of Poker Champion Tom McEvoy was born in Grand Rapids, Michigan.

1945 – Richard Nixon, while playing 5-Card Draw during the War in the South Pacific, held the A♦ and drew the T♦, J♦, Q♦ and K♦ to make a royal flush. The odds against that draw are 650,000-1 against.

1945, June 1st – When Harry S Truman became President upon the death of FDR on April 12th he didn't leave the White House a single time for six weeks. When he did leave for the first time, it was to go to a poker game.

1945, August 2nd – President Harry S Truman played pot limit poker with the press corps sixteen hours a day aboard ship while coming home from the Potsdam Conference.

1945-1953—Poker chips used in the White House for President Truman's poker games had the Presidential Seal embellished on them.

1945, December 6th – 1995 World Series of Poker Champion Dan Harrington was born in Cambridge, Massachusetts.

1946 – John Von Neumann and Osker Morganstern published *Theory of Games and Economic Behavior*. This was the creation of a new field of study called game theory.

"Son, no matter how far you travel, or how smart you get,
always remember this: Some day, somewhere, a guy is going
to come to you and show you a nice brand-new deck of cards,
on which the seal is never broken, and this guy is going to

offer to bet you that the jack of spades will jump out of this
deck and squirt cider in your ear. But, son, do not bet him,
for as sure as you do you are going to get an ear full of cider.

Damon Runyon
The Idylls of Miss Sarah Brown, 1946

1946 – Benny Binion left Dallas, Texas for good because, as he said, it was "the year that my sheriff got beat in the election."

1946, December 31st—Duane "Dewey" Tomko was born in Glassport, Pennsylvania.

1948 – Johnny Moss opened the first Las Vegas poker rooms on the Strip, at the Golden Nugget and the Dunes. The rake was 10% of the pot with no maximum. He also hired the first female poker dealers ever in Las Vegas.

1949 – Nick "The Greek" Dandalos and Johnny Moss play a five-month long head-up poker game in Las Vegas. This game was the inspiration for the inception of what was to become the World Series of Poker.

Mr. Moss, I have to let you go.

Nick "The Greek" Dandalos, after losing close to $4,000,000 to Johnny Moss in the previous five months. 1949

The next best thing to playing and winning is
playing and losing. The main thing is to play.

Nick "The Greek" Dandalos, 1949

1949 – Physicist Albert Einstein visited Las Vegas during the Moss vs. Dandalos poker match. He was introduced around town as "Little Al from Jersey."

1949 – Puggy Pearson is the person credited with being the originator of the idea of a freeze-out type poker tournament.

There were few women gamblers in those days,
for women have too many nerves; there are too

*many temptations which make them display their
emotions—feminine instinct prohibits the usual
poker face. One must have a countenance that
remains immovable hour after hour.*

Poker Alice Tubbs, 1949

1950 – 1978 World Series of Poker Champion Bobby Baldwin was born in Ardmore, Oklahoma.

Poker and American history are inseparable.

John McDonald, 1950

1950s – "Snatch games" were the norm in Las Vegas. Dealers would take the 10% rake from the pot and then surreptitiously 'snatch' as much more money as they could from the pot without arousing the suspicion of the players.

Bluff enough to get caught half the time.

George Coffin
The Poker Game Complete, 1950

1951, July 5th – 1991 World Series of Poker Champion Brad Daugherty was born in Mountain Grove, Missouri.

*I would rather play poker with five or six
experts than to eat.*

Poker Alice, 1951

1951 – Benny Binion bought the El Dorado and Apache Casinos and renamed them the Horseshoe. He was the first Las Vegas casino owner to put carpet on the gambling floor of the casino, dispatch limousines to the airport to accommodate high rollers and the first to give free drinks to gamblers.

1952 – 1993 World Series of Poker Champion Jim Bechtel was born.

1953, September 8th – 1980, 1981 and 1997 World Series of Poker Champion Stu Ungar was born.

> *The more wild cards and crazy rules,*
> *the greater the expert's advantage.*
>
> John R. Crawford, 1953

1955 – Movie star John Wayne won the equally famous dog Lassie from her (all of the dogs who played Lassie were female) owner and trainer during a poker game. He later gave the dog back.

1955 – Nevada created the Gaming Control Board under the direction of the State Treasury Division.

1955 – Vice President Richard Nixon, defending President Eisenhower's considerable time spent on the golf course, said, "If the President spent as much time playing golf as Truman spent playing poker, the President would be able to beat Ben Hogan."

1956 – Women poker players or spectators were not allowed in Las Vegas poker rooms before this year.

1957 – 1987 and 1988 World Series of Poker Champion Johnny Chan was born.

> *Never play cards with a man named Doc.*
>
> Nelson Algren, 1957

1957, November 9th – The *Saturday Evening Post* published an excerpt called *Winning at Poker* from Herbert O. Yardley's book *The Education of a Poker Player*. The paper broke all newsstand records when the edition sold 5,600,000 copies.

1958, August 7th – Herbert O. Yardley died at age 69.

1959, January 16th – 1996 World Series of Poker Champion Huckleberry Seed was born.

1959 – Nevada created the Nevada Gaming Commission to oversee decisions of the Gaming Control Board.

1961, October 7th – 2002 World Series of Poker Champion Robert Varkonyi was born.

If you know poker, you know people; and
if you know people, you got the whole dang
world lined up in your sights.

James Garner, as Bret Maverick, 1962

1962, October 28th – 1998 World Series of Poker Champion Scotty Nguyen was born in Nha Trang, Vietnam.

1963, April 11th – 2000 World Series of Poker Champion Chris Ferguson was born in Los Angeles, California.

1963 – Texas Hold'em was first introduced to Las Vegas poker rooms by Texan Felton "Corky" McCorquodale.

At the card game, one of the boys looked across
the table and said, "Now Reuben, play the cards
fair. I know what I dealt you.

Lyndon B. Johnson

1963, November 25th—On this, the day that President John F. Kennedy was buried, all gambling in Las Vegas has halted from 7 a.m. to midnight.

1964 – The Gambler's Book Shop was opened in Las Vegas by John and Edna Luckman. The bookstore's motto is "Knowledge is Protection."

1964, June 25th – 2004 World Series of Poker Champion Greg Raymer was born in Minot, North Dakota.

1964, July 16th – 1989 World Series of Poker Champion Phil Hellmuth, Jr. was born in Madison, Wisconsin.

For the true gambler, money is never an end in itself.
It's a tool, like language or thought.

Steve McQueen, as The Kid,
The Cincinnati Kid movie, 1965

1965—In the *Cincinnati Kid* movie, Steve McQueen's character plays a hand of heads-up poker against Edward G. Robinson's character. He makes a full house, Aces full of Tens, and loses to Robinson's Queen-high straight flush. The odds against that are 332,220,508,616 to 1.

1966 – Don Laughlin opened the Riverside Resort Hotel & Casino, in Laughlin, Nevada. It was the first casino in town.

1966, November 3rd – 2005 World Series of Poker champion Joseph Hachem was born in Lebanon.

The first rule of poker is, whether you play by
Western or Eastern rules, is put up or shut up!

Henry Fonda
A Big Hand for the Little Lady, 1966

1966, December 25th—Nick 'the Greek' Dandalos died at age 77 in Los Angeles, California.

1968 – 2007 World Series of Poker Champion Xao "Jerry" Yang was born in Laos.

1969, January 15th – 1996 World Series of Poker Champion Huckleberry "Huck" Seed was born.

1969 – Nevada legalized the ownership of casinos by public corporations.

1969 – Benny Binion hosted a high stakes poker game at the Holiday Hotel during the Texas Gambler's Reunion in Reno, Nevada. They played poker for six or seven days and Johnny Moss was named the "King of Cards" and presented with a silver cup. This event got several of the participants thinking about what could be, and next year the event was held in Las Vegas and was known as the first world series of poker.

1969, August 25th – 2002 World Series of Poker Champion Jamie Gold was born in Kansas City, Missouri.

1969—Future Speaker of the House of Representatives Congressman Tip O'Neill told President Richard M. Nixon, "You know, I'm sick and tired of reading what a good poker player you are. As a matter of fact, you're one of the worst poker players I've ever seen."

WORLD SERIES OF POKER (WSOP) FINAL HAND ACTION, SUMMARIES, STATISTICS AND TRIVIA

1970
1st WORLD SERIES OF POKER
Johnny "Grand Old Man of Poker" Moss

There is no video record of the 1970 WSOP. Thirty-eight players gathered to play five different card games. Those games were 5-Card Stud, 7-Card Stud, Deuce-to-7 Lowball, Razz and Texas Hold'em. Veteran pro Johnny Moss was the winner in all five events and was voted the winner. There was no runner-up.

Because Binion's Horseshoe didn't have a poker room, the baccarat tables were replaced with three poker tables.

Of the thirty-seven total players, seven professional poker players competed in the first WSOP main event:

Johnny Moss
Doyle Brunson
Sailor Roberts
Amarillo Slim Preston
Puggy Pearson
Crandell Addington
Carl Cannon

Of these seven players, the first five would go on to win WSOP main event titles, the sixth would finish in second place twice and all of the first six would be voted into the Poker Hall of Fame.

The average age of the players at the main event final table was 45 year old.

The events at the first WSOP consisted of:

5-Card Draw

5-Card Stud
7-Card Stud
7-Card Stud, High-Low 8/Better
No-Limit Texas Hold'em

The first WSOP Champion was determined by a vote of the seven players. The first secret ballot was a 7-way tie—each player had voted for himself! After being told they would have to vote for another player besides themselves, Johnny Moss won in a 6-1 landslide. The only player not to vote for Johnny Moss was Johnny Moss!

Johnny Moss was awarded a silver cup for his win.

Jack Straus was voted "Most Congenial."

The two-card Texas Hold'em starting hand Ace-Ten is called "The Johnny Moss."

Johnny Moss went on to play in every WSOP from 1970 to 1995.

Never play poker with a guy named after
a city or a guy named Doc.

Poker Wisdom

1970 – There were only 70 licensed poker tables in Nevada. They took in $4,500,000 ($64,285 per table) that year.

1971
2ND WORLD SERIES OF POKER
Johnny "Grand Old Man of Poker" Moss

Six players paid $5,000 each to enter the tournament. They were Johnny Moss, Walker Clyde "Puggy" Pearson, Sailor Roberts, Jack Straus, Doyle Brunson and long ago faded into poker obscurity Jimmy Casella. He would be the only one of the six to not eventually win a WSOP Championship. Johnny Moss won the entire $30,000 entry main event prize pool. The runner-up was Puggy Pearson, who won no prize money for that distinction. Little known is the fact that Bob Hooks finished in third place.

The preliminary events, each paying $10,000, leading up to the main event were:

Limit 7-Card Stud, won by Puggy Pearson
Limit Razz, won by Jimmy Casella
Limit 5-Card Stud, won by Bill Boyd
Limit Ace to Five Draw, won by Johnny Moss

*Owing largely to the bluff, poker has influenced
our thinking on life, love, business and war.
In fact, mathematical theory of games... was
given a high security classification by the
armed forces during World War II.*

A.D. Livingston, 1971

1972
3RD WORLD SERIES OF POKER
Thomas "Amarillo Slim" Preston

The 1972 WSOP was won by Thomas "Amarillo Slim" Preston. This was the first year that the entry fee was $10,000. He defeated seven other players to win the entire $80,000 entry prize pool. The runner-up was Walter Clyde "Puggy" Pearson. Tournament organizer Benny Binion was so worried that the new $10,000 buy-in would hurt the tournament's popularity, he personally paid half of everyone's buy-in.

The winner of the 1972 WSOP was determined by a deal made between the final three players. Being a seriously religious man, Doyle Brunson didn't want to be known as "The World Champion of Poker." He then cashed out his chips for $20,000, saying he was too sick to play any further. Pearson didn't want to attract the attention of the Internal Revenue Service. Amarillo Slim Preston then became the champion by default.

The results of the 1972 WSOP main event were:

1st	Thomas "Amarillo Slim" Preston	$60,000
2nd	Walter "Puggy" Pearson	None
3rd	Doyle Brunson	$20,000
4th	Crandell Addington	None
5th	Jack Straus	None
6th	Johnny Moss	None
7th	Roger Van Ausdall	None
8th	Jimmy Casella	None

This was the first and only time that 3rd place paid more than 2nd place in the WSOP.

When he died, Benny Binion left his horse to Amarillo Slim.

Slim says he receives all mail addressed to him at: "Amarillo Slim, Amarillo, Texas." (Author's note: How would he know what mail he doesn't receive?)

1972, April 13th – 2001 World Series of Poker Champion Juan Carlos Mortensen was born.

> *You can shear a sheep many*
> *times but you can only skin 'em once.*

> Amarillo Slim Preston, 1972

1972 –*The Advanced Concepts of Poker,* by Frank R. Wallace was published. It became the biggest-selling poker book in the world up to this date.

1973
4TH WORLD SERIES OF POKER
Walter Clyde "Puggy" Pearson

Winner: Walter Clyde "Puggy" Pearson
Runner-up: Johnny Moss

| # of Players: | 13 |
| Prize: | $130,000 |

The Final Hand:

Odds:		Pre-flop	Flop	Turn
Pearson	A♠ 7♠	59.19	65.96	75.00
Board:	2♣ T♠ Q♠ 5♥ 6♦			
Moss	K♥ J♠	40.33	34.04	25.0

This was a re-match of the 1971 WSOP final table, which Moss won. Pearson won this one. Moss shouldn't be faulted too much—he was sixty-eight years old at the time. Thirteen players each paid $10,000 to enter the main event. All of the prize money went to 1st place.

The final table was:

1st	Puggy Pearson	$130,000
2nd	Johnny Moss	None
3rd	Jack Straus	None
4th	Bobby Brazil	None
5th	Bob Hooks	None
6th	Sailor Roberts	None

The rest of the WSOP's event winners were:

$1,000 7-Card Razz	Sam Angel	$32,000
$3,000 2-7 Draw	Aubrey Day	$16,500
$1,000 No Limit Hold'em	Puggy Pearson	$17,000
$4,000 7-Card Stud	Puggy Pearson	$32,000
$3,000 2-7 Draw	Jack Straus	$16,500
Limit Ace to Five Draw	Joe Bernstein	$21,000
5-Card Stud	Bill Boyd	$10,000

Puggy Pearson is a former U.S. Navy frogman.

Vera, if you can win the WSOP, you can
take a dull knife and cut my throat!

Amarillo Slim Preston
To Vera Richmond, 1973

(Often misquoted as "If a woman ever wins the WSOP, I'll slit my throat with a knife.)

Benny Binion said, "We had 13 players this year. I look to have better than 20 players next year. It's likely to even get up to 50. Might get to be more than that. It will, eventually."

Puggy Pearson was a scratch golfer.

Puggy Pearson is the only person to play in every WSOP from 1970 to 2005.

Puggy's winning hand was only Ace-high.

Aces are larger than life
and greater than mountains.

Mike Caro

If I lose today, I can look forward to winning tomorrow,
and if I win today, I can expect to lose tomorrow.
A sure thing is no fun.

Chico Marx, 1973

1973 – CBS Sports televised the WSOP for the first time. Jimmy "The Greek" Snyder narrated the final showdown between Johnny Moss and Puggy Pearson. The action was taped live but not shown on television until it aired on *Sports Spectacular* a few weeks later.

1974
5TH WORLD SERIES OF POKER
Johnny "Grand Old Man of Poker" Moss

Winner: Johnny Moss
Runner-up   Crandell Addington
# of Players: 16
Prize: $160,000

The player's hole cards and community cards on the board for the final winning hand for Johnny Moss are unknown.

The final table was:

1st	Johnny Moss	$160,000
2nd	Crandell Addington	None
3rd	Unknown	None
4th	Bob Hooks	None
5th	Unknown	None
6th	Unknown	None

Other players at the final table were Amarillo Slim Preston, Doyle Brunson, Sailor Roberts, Puggy Pearson and Jimmy Casella.

The rest of the WSOP's events winners were:

$5,000 5-Card Stud	Bill Boyd	$40,000
$1,000 7-Card Razz	Jimmy Casella	$25,000
$10,000 7-Card Stud	Jimmy Casella	$41,225
$1,000 No Limit Hold'em	Amarillo Slim Preston	$11,100
$5,000 2-7 Draw	Sailor Roberts	$35,850

Johnny Moss received the first bracelet given to a main event champion. It was from Neiman-Marcus.

Amarillo Slim appeared in the movie *California Split*.

Crandell Addington became the first player (followed by T.J. Cloutier and Dewey Tomko) to be a two-time WSOP main event runner-up. Again, there was no second-prize money in this event.

The buffets at the early WSOP events featured bear meat, rattlesnake meat and buffalo steak.

As of 2009, Johnny Moss is only one of two three-time winners of the WSOP. The other is Stu Ungar.

> *If you want to be a professional poker player, there*
> *is no elevator to the top. You have to take the stairs.*

> Ken Warren, 2003

1975
6TH WORLD SERIES OF POKER
Brian "Sailor" Roberts

Winner: Sailor Roberts
Runner-up: Bob Hooks
# of Players: 21
Prize: $210,000

The final Hand:

Odds:		Pre-flop
Roberts	9♠ 9♥	55.53

The Board:	Unknown

Hooks	A♣ K	44.16

The final table was:

1st	Brian "Sailor" Roberts	$210,000
2nd	Bob Hooks	None

3rd	Crandell Addington	None
4th	Aubrey Day	None
5th	Unknown	None
6th	Jesse Alto	None

The rest of the WSOP's events winners were:

$1,000 7-Card Razz	Sam Angel	$17,000
$1,000 2-7 Draw	Billy Baxter	$35,000
$5,000 No Limit Hold'em	Jay Heimowitz	$32,000
$1,000 7-Card Stud	Johnny Moss	$44,000

All event winners were awarded a sterling plate.

Sailor Roberts was also (in 1982) the first, but not the last, WSOP Champion to become a drug-abuse fatality.

5-Card Stud was dropped from the WSOP schedule this year.

1975, November 21st – 2003 World Series of Poker Champion Christopher "Chris" Moneymaker was born.

Poker is a tough way to make an easy living.

Poker Wisdom

1875 to 1975 – Only 128 poker books were written in the entire world, with 93 being published in the United States and 22 being published in England.

1976
7TH WORLD SERIES OF POKER
Doyle "Texas Dolly" Brunson

Winner: Doyle Brunson
Runner-up: Jesse Alto

# of Players: 22
Prize: $220,000

The Final Hand:

Odds:		PF	Flop	Turn
Brunson	T♠ 2♠	34.14	11.92	9.09

The Board: A♥ J♠ T♥ 2♣ T♦

Alto	A♠ J♥	65.33	86.67	90.91

The final table was:

1st	Doyle Brunson	$220,000
2nd	Jesse Alto	None
3rd	Tommy Hufnagle	None
4th	Crandell Addington	None
5th	Bob Hooks	None

The other players at the final table were Howard "Tahoe" Andrew, Amarillo Slim Preston, Johnny Moss, Jimmy Casella, and Sailor Roberts.

The rest of the WSOP's events winners were:

$2,500 No Limit Hold'em	"Tahoe" Andrew	$28,000
$1,000 No Limit Hold'em	"Tahoe" Andrew	$23,600
$1,00 Ace to Five Draw	Perry Green	$68,300
$5,000 2-7 Draw w/Rebuys	Doyle Brunson	$80,250
$500 7-Card Stud	Johnny Moss	$13,000
$1,000 7-Card Stud Split	Doc Green	Unknown
$5,000 7-Card Stud	Walter Smiley	$35,000

This is the first year that the WSOP started the tradition of awarding bracelets to all event winners.

Doyle Brunson got his nickname "Texas Dolly" when event moderator "Jimmy the Greek" Snyder mispronounced his name.

As a college student, Doyle was a member of the Texas All-State Basketball team and was chosen as one of the ten best basketball players in the country. He was about to be drafted by the Minneapolis Lakers when his leg was crushed in a summer job accident.

While in college, Doyle ran the one-mile event in 4:43.

Doyle Brunson holds a Master's Degree in Administrative Education.

Doyle says he lost his entire six-figure bankroll during his first-ever trip to Las Vegas.

It's not the hands you play, it's the hands you fold
that determine whether or not you'll have a positive bottom line.

Doyle Brunson

1976, February 1st—Phil Ivey was born in Riverside, California.

1976 – Walter Smiley, a Gardena, California professional poker player, became the first African-American to win a WSOP bracelet when he won the $5,000 buy-in 7-Card Stud event.

1976 – November 2nd – New Jersey voters, by a vote of 56% to 44%, voted to legalize casino-style gambling in Atlantic City.

1976 – The first book devoted entirely to the game of Texas Hold'em, *Hold'em Poker,* was written by David Sklansky. The cover price was $2.00.

1976 – The first video poker machine was installed in a Las Vegas casino. It was a black & white video but a color machine was invented only eight months later.

1977
8TH WORLD SERIES OF POKER
Doyle "Texas Dolly" Brunson

Winner: Doyle Brunson
Runner-up: Gary "Bones" Berland

| # of Players: | 34 |
| Prize: | $340,000 |

The Final Hand:

Odds:		Pre-flop/	Flop/	Turn
Brunson	T♠ 2♥	55.58	25.45	90.91

Board:	T♦ 8♠ 5♥ 2♣ T♣			

| Berland | 8♥ 5♣ | 42.38 | 74.55 | 9.09 |

The final table was:

1st	Doyle Brunson	$340,000
2nd	Gary "Bones" Berland	None
3rd	Milo Jacobson	None
4th	Andy Moore	None
5th	Sailor Roberts	None

The rest of the WSOP's events winners were:

$500 Ace to Five Draw	Billy Allen	$10,800
$10 2-7 Draw	Bobby Baldwin	$80,000
$5,000 7-Card Stud	Bobby Baldwin	$44,000
$500 7-Card Razz	Gary "Bones" Berland	$8,300
$1,000 7-Card Stud Split	Doyle Brunson	$62,500
$5,000 Ace to Five Draw	Perry Green	$10,000
$1,000 No Limit Hold'em	George Huber	$33,000
$1,500 No Limit Hold'em	Louis Hunsucker	$34,200
$100 Ladies 7-Card Stud	Jackie McDaniels	$5,580
$1,000 7-Card Stud Split	Fats Morgan	$10,800
$500 7-Card Stud	Jeff Sandow	$11,400
$5,000 7-Card Stud	Richard Schwartz	$25,000

Doyle Brunson won the WSOP while holding a 10-2 offsuit in both 1976 and 1977. Both years he flopped a pair of tens, and was still behind, made two pair on the turn and a full house on the river.

Doyle's book *Super/System* originally sold for $100 a copy. The subtitle is *How I Made Over $1,000,000 Playing Poker*. He has since suggested that a revised subtitle might be *How I Lost Over $1,000,000 Playing Golf*.

Next year's WSOP Champion Bobby Baldwin cashed in the WSOP for the first time by winning the Deuce to Seven Draw and 7-Card Stud events.

The first ladies' only tournament, The Women's Championship of Poker made its debut this year. The winner was Jackie McDaniels, who won $5,580 in the 7-Card Stud event.

1978
9TH WORLD SERIES OF POKER
Bobby "The Owl" Baldwin

Winner: Bobby Baldwin
Runner-up: Crandell Addington
#of Players: 42
Prize: $210,000

The Final Hand:

Odds:		Preflop/	Flop/	Turn
Baldwin	Q♦ Q♣	81.63	94.04	97.73
Board:	Q♠ 9♥ K♣ A♠ T♦			
Addington	9♦ 9♣	17.9	4.34	2.27

The final table was:

1st	Bobby Baldwin	$210,000
2nd	Crandell Addington	$84,000
3rd	Louis Hunsucker	$63,000
4th	Buck Buchanan	$42,000
5th	Jesse Alto	$21,000
6th	Ken Smith	None

The rest of the WSOP's events winners were:

$10,000 2-7 Draw	Billy Baxter	$90,000
$1,000 7-Card Razz	Gary Berland	$19,200
$500 7-Card Stud	Gary Berland	$17,100
$5,000 7-Card Stud	Doyle Brunson	$68,000
$1,000 No Limit Hold'em	Aubrey Day	$42,600
$200 Ladies' 7-Card Stud	Terry King	$10,800
$5,000 Draw High	Lakewood Louie	$21,000
$1,500 No Limit Hold'em	Hans "Tuna" Lund	$46,800
$1,000 7-Card Stud Split	David "Chip" Reese	$22,200
$1,000 Ace to Five Draw	Henry Young	$19,200

For the first time, the main event was not a winner-take-all event. The prize money was split among the final five players as: 50% for 1st, 20% for 2nd, 15% for 3rd, 10% for 4th and 5% for 5th.

Bobby Baldwin won the Championship when his set of Queens held up against Addington's set of 9s.

After calling Baldwin's bet that put him all-in, Addington took a poker chip off Baldwin's stack, used it for a card cover and said, "I may have to borrow that to get home on."

After flopping a set of 9s and losing the championship, Crandell Addington, ever the gentleman, shook Bobby Baldwin's hand and said, "That's the way I wanted to go out."

Playing a winning rush usually gives momentum
to all of the elements of winning play.

Bobby Baldwin, 1984

When he won the title, Bobby Baldwin was wearing a light-green long-sleeve shirt that was unbuttoned nearly down to his navel. Dark, overflowing chest hair complemented his large, curly Afro-like hairdo. A photograph taken at this moment was placed in its place of honor next to the photos of the other WSOP Champions in Binion's Horseshoe.

Years later, after he became CEO of a large Las Vegas casino, that photo of Bobby Baldwin was quietly replaced with a professional studio-quality photograph of himself wearing an expensive suit and tie, with a clean-shaven face and a proper conservative businessman's haircut befitting an insecure, albeit serious-looking businessman.

Actor Gabe Kaplan, of *Welcome Back, Kotter* fame, was the fourth player busted out of the tournament, out of 42 entrants.

The first woman ever to enter the WSOP main event was Barbara Freer.

Bobby Baldwin is the youngest-yet winner of the WSOP, at age 28.

1988, May 26 – Resorts International became the first legal casino in eastern North America.

My father once told me never to bet on
anything but Notre Dame and the Yankees.

New Jersey Governor Brendan Byrne
Cutting ribbon to open Resorts Casino

1979
10TH WORLD SERIES OF POKER
Hal Fowler

Winner:	Hal Fowler
Runner-up:	Bobby Hoff
# of Players:	54
Prize:	$270,000

The Final Hand:

Odds:		Pre-flop/	Flop/	Turn
Fowler	7♠ 6♦	19.22	20.3	100.00

60

Board: J♠ 3♣ 5♥ 4♠ T♦

Hoff   A♥ A♣   80.52   79.7   00.00

The final table was:

1ˢᵗ	Hal Fowler	$270,000
2ⁿᵈ	Bobby Hoff	$108,000
3ʳᵈ	George Huber	$81,000
4ᵗʰ	Sam Moon	$54,000
5ᵗʰ	Johnny Moss	$27,000
6ᵗʰ	David "Chip" Reese	None
7ᵗʰ	Sam Petrillo	None
8ᵗʰ	Crandell Addington	None
9ᵗʰ	Bobby Baldwin	None

The rest of the WSOP's events winners were:

$10,000 2-7 Draw	Bobby Baldwin	$90,000
$500 7-Card Stud	Gary Berland	$24,000
$1,000 7-Card Stud	Gary Berland	$20,400
$600 Mixed Doubles	Doyle Brunson & Starla Brodie	$4,500
$400 Ladies' 7-Card Stud	Barbara Freer	$12,720
$1,500 No Limit Hold'em	Perry Green	$76,500
$1,000 Ace to Five Draw	Lakewood Louie	$22,200
$2,000 Draw High	Lakewood Louie	$22,800
$1,000 Razz	Sam Mastrogiannis	$22,200
$5,000 7-Card Stud	Johnny Moss	$48,000
$1,000 No Limit Hold'em	Dewey Tomko	$48,000

Two female players entered the WSOP this year.

Hal Fowler is the first amateur to win the WSOP.

Hal Fowler's win over professional Bobby Hoff is to this day considered to be the biggest upset in WSOP history.

Hal Fowler also had Johnny Moss and Bobby Baldwin at his final table, and he still won the title.

After getting head-up, play lasted for more than five hours, until 2:58am.

Future WSOP Champion Jack Straus was the first player eliminated, out of 54 entrants.

Actor-turned-commentator Gabe Kaplan was the sixth player eliminated.

"Lakewood Louie" was the first player in WSOP history to make a royal flush (while holding K♦T♦).

1978 WSOP Champion Bobby Baldwin busted out in 8th place when he held pocket 8s against pocket Aces. He flopped an 8, went all in, and lost the hand when an Ace came on the turn.

Johnny Moss busted out in fifth place while holding A♠Q♣. He lost to an A♥T♦.

At the final table, eventual winner Hal Fowler at one point had only 1,700 chips out of a total 540,000 chips on the table. That's less than one-third of one percent of the chips.

Entertainer Kenny Rogers personally appeared at this year's WSOP to sing his new blockbuster hit *The Gambler*. Released on November 15th 1978, it hit #1 on the country charts and #16 on the pop charts.

1979 – The Poker Hall of Fame was established. The standards for getting into the Poker Hall of Fame are:

1. Nominee must have played poker against acknowledged top competition,
2. Played for high stakes,
3. Played consistently well and gained the respect of his peers
4. Stood the test of time, and
5. Or, for non-players, contributed to the overall growth and success of the game of poker, with indelible positive and lasting results.

The first seven inductees were:

Johnny Moss (1907-1995)
Nick "The Greek" Dandalos (1883-1966)
Felton "Corky" McCorquodale (?-?)
Red Winn (?-?)

Sid Wyman (1910-1978)
James Butler "Wild Bill" Hickok (1837-1876)
Edmond Hoyle (1672-1769)

The Poker hall of Fame was acquired by Harrah's Entertainment in 2004. There are 16 living members. Wild Bill Hickok, Jack "Treetop" Straus and Tommy Abdo are three members who died while playing poker.

1980
11TH WORLD SERIES OF POKER
Stuart "Stuey The Kid" Ungar

Winner: Stu Ungar
Runner-Up: Doyle Brunson
# of Players: 73
Prize: $385,000

The Final Hand:

Odds:		Pre-flop	Flop	Turn
Ungar:	5♠ 4♠	38.9	17.78	90.91
Board:	A♦ 7♦ 2♣ 3♥ 2♦			
Brunson	A♥ 7♥	60.57	82.22	9.09

The final table was:

1st	Stu Ungar	$385,000
2nd	Doyle Brunson	$146,000
3rd	Jay Hiemowitz	$109,500
4th	Johnny Moss	$73,000
5th	Charles Dunwoody	$36,500
6th	Gabe Kaplan	None

The rest of the WSOP's events winners were:

$1,000 7-Card Stud Split	Mickey Appleman	$30,800
$1,000 No Limit Hold'em	Robert Bone	$69,000
$2,000 Draw High	Pat Callihan	$15,600
$400 Ladies' 7-Card Stud	Debby Callihan	$14,880
$5,000 7-Card Stud	Peet Chris	$90,000
$10,000 2-7 Draw	Sarge Ferris	$150,000
$1,500 No Limit Hold'em	Gene Fisher	$113,400
$1,000 Ace to Five Draw	Jim Fugatti	$35,600
$600 Mixed Doubles	A.J. Myers & Lynn Harvey	$7,380
$500 7-Card Stud	Bobby Schwing	$52,800
$1,000 7-Card Stud	Lakewood Louie	$33,600

Stu Ungar had never played Texas Hold'em in his life until this year. He was such a superior gin rummy player (he won a gin tournament against adults at age 10) that he couldn't get any action in New York. So he came to Las Vegas to take up poker.

Doyle Brunson later said that if anyone had taken Stu out on Day 1, he (Brunson) could not have lost the title.

Brunson not only lost to Ungar in the head-up final table, but also lost a $50,000 side bet to him.

Stu Ungar was so good at counting cards that he was banned from playing Blackjack (21) in Las Vegas.

Stu Ungar won a $100,000 bet against casino owner Bob Stupak that he could count down a six-deck shoe of cards and name the exact last card in the shoe.

Stu Ungar never had a social security number in his life until this year, when he needed to get one to claim his WSOP winnings.

Positive identification is required to enter the WSOP; however, a birth certificate is not required.

Stu Ungar won more than $30,000,000 in his lifetime playing poker.

A genuine smile usually means a genuine hand;
a forced smile is a bluff.

Mike Caro, 1984

1980 – There were 423 licensed poker tables in Nevada casinos. They earned $50,164,000 ($118,591 per table) that year.

1980 – T. "Blondie" Forbes was inducted into the Poker Hall of Fame.

1980s – WSOP bracelets were made by Las Vegas jeweler Mordechai Yerushalmi until Harrah's Entertainment bought the rights in 2004.

1981
12ᵀᴴ WORLD SERIES OF POKER
Stu "Stuey, The Kid" Ungar

Winner:	Stu Ungar
Runner-up:	Perry Green
# of Players:	75
Prize:	$375,000

The Final Hand:

Odds:		Pre-flop/	Flop/	Turn
Ungar	A♥ Q♥	60.68	12.73	6.82
Board:	8♥ 7♦ 4♥ 4♠ Q♦			
Green	T♣ 9♦	34.58	28.38	22.73

The final table was:

1st	Stu Ungar	$375,000
2nd	Perry Green	$150,000
3rd	Gene Fisher	$75,000
4th	Ken Smith	$37,500

5th	Bill Smith	$37,500
6th	Jay Hiemowitz	$30,000

The rest of the WSOP's events winners were:

$1,000 Draw High	Ed Barmach	$18,000
$600 Mixed Doubles	Frank Cardone & Juanda Matthews	$7,800
$1,500 No Limit Hold'em	Fredric David	$96,000
$1,000 7-Card Stud	Sid Gammerman	$52,000
$400 Ladies 7-Card Stud	Ruth Godfrey	$17,600
$1,000 7-Card Razz	Bruce Hershenson	$34,000
$1,000 7-Card Stud Split	Johnny Moss	$33,500
$5,000 7-Card Stud	A.J. Myers	$67,500
$2,500 Ace to Five Draw	Mickey Perry	$46,250
$1,000 Ace to Five Draw	Dudy Roach	$81,000
$10,000 2-7 Draw	Stu Ungar	$95,000

For the first time, the WSOP awarded prize money to all six players who made the final table.

When the final table got down to six-handed, Amarillo Slim proposed a "Texans versus Jews" bet, as there were three of each at the table. Stu Ungar won his second consecutive title and the *Welcome Back, Kotter* star won the side bet.

1981, May – America's Cup Poker Tournament – After making the final table Johnny Chan knocked out all eight of his opponents in less than one hour. Bob Stupak remarked that he was the "Orient Express" of poker. He's been known as Johnny "The Orient Express" Chan ever since.

Stu Ungar went from millionaire to broke four times, dying broke.

I like to play poker with politicians. They're easy to beat....sometimes in poker it's smarter to lose with a winning hand so that you can win later with a losing hand. Politicians can't accept that.

Robert Redford
Havana, 1990

1981 – Bill Boyd was inducted into the Poker Hall of Fame.

1981—The Irish Poker Open held their first tournament. It is the longest-running No Limit Texas Hold'em poker tournament in Europe and it's the second-longest running after the WSOP.

1982
13TH WORLD SERIES OF POKER
Jack "Treetop" Straus

Winner: Jack "Treetop" Straus
Runner-up: Dewey Tomko
# of Players: 104
Prize: $520,000

The Final Hand:

Odds:		Pre-flop/	Flop/	Turn
Straus	A♥ T♣	60.68	12.73	6.82
Board:	6♦ 5♠ 4♠ Q♣ T♠			
Tomko	A♦ 4♦	29.09	81.82	93.18

The final table was:

1st	Jack Straus	$520,000
2nd	Dewey Tomko	$208,000
3rd	Berry Johnston	$104,000
4th	Doyle Brunson	$52,000
5th	A.J. Myers	$52,000
6th	Dudy Roach	$41,000
7th	Unknown	None
8th	Sailor Roberts	None

The rest of the WSOP's preliminary event winners were:

$2,500 Ace to Five Draw	Billy Baxter	$48,750
$10,000 2-7 Seven Draw	Billy Baxter	$95,000
$1,000 7-Card Stud Split	Tom Cress	$44,000
$1,000 No Limit Hold'em	Jim Doman	$96,000
$500 Ladies 7-Card Stud	June Field	$16,000
$1,000 7-Card Razz	Nick Helm	$40,000
$800 Mixed Doubles	David Sklansky & Dani Kelly	$8,800
$1,500 No Limit Hold'em	Ralph Morton	$123,000
$1,000 No Limit Hold'em	John Paquette	$101,000
$5,000 7-Card Stud	Chip Reese	$92,500
$1,000 Ace to Five Draw	Vera Richmond	$38,500
$1,000 Draw High	David Sklansky	$15,000
$1,000 7-Card Stud	Don Williams	$56,000

WSOP winner Jack Straus was the inspiration for the tournament phrase "a chip and a chair." On Day 1 of the tournament, he called with all his chips and lost the hand. As he was about to leave, a single $500 chip was discovered under his cocktail napkin. Since he had not declared himself to be all-in, he was allowed to keep the chip and continue to play. He doubled up on the next two hands, and we know how the tournament turned out after that.

Jack Straus was 6"6' tall, hence the nickname Treetop.

Vera Richmond became the first woman to win a WSOP bracelet, winning the Ace to 5 Draw event, and $38,500.

1975 World Series of Poker Champion Sailor Roberts made the final table and died later in the year.

A Smith & Wesson beats four Aces.

Poker Wisdom

If there's no risk in losing, there's no high in winning.
I have only a limited amount of time on this earth, and
I want to live every second of if. That's why I'm willing
to play anyone in the world for any amount.

Jack Straus, 1983

1982 – This is the first year that Omaha was played in a Las Vegas casino. Golden Nugget Casino executive Robert Turner learned about the game from a female visitor from Seattle. After explaining to him that it had been a popular home game in the Seattle area since 1978, he introduced it into his poker room as "Nugget Hold'em."

1982 – Tommy Abdo was enshrined in The Poker Hall of Fame.

1983
14TH WORLD SERIES OF POKER
Thomas K. "Tom" McEvoy

1983, May 12th
Winner: Tom McEvoy
Runner-up: Rod Peate
# of Players: 108
Prize: $540,000

The Final Hand:

Odds:		Pre-flop/	Flop/	Turn
McEvoy	Q♥ Q♠	67.48	83.54	88.64
Board:	6♦ 6♥ 9♣ 8♠ J♦			
Peate	K♦ J♦	32.14	16.46	11.36

The final table was:

1st	Tom McEvoy	$540,000
2nd	Rod Peate	$216,000
3rd	Doyle Brunson	$108,000
4th	Carl McKelvey	$54,000
5th	Robert Geers	$54,000
6th	Donnacha O'Dea	$43,200
7th	John Squatty	$21,600
8th	R.R. Pennington	$21,600
9th	George Huber	$21,600

The rest of the WSOP's events winners were:

$2,500 Ace to Five Draw	David Angel	$46,250
$1,500 No Limit Hold'em	David Baxter	$145,250
$1,000 7-Card Stud Split	Artie Cobb	$52,000
$800 Mixed Doubles	Jim & Donna Doman	$10,000
$1,000 7-Card Stud	Ken Flaton	$62,000
$500 Ladies' 7-Card Stud	Carolyn Gardner	$16,000
$1,000 No Limit Hold'em	Buster Jackson	$124,000
$2,500 Match Play	Berry Johnston	$40,000
$1,000 7-Card Razz	John Lucas	$43,000
$1,000 Limit Hold'em	Tom McEvoy	$117,000
$1,000 Limit Omaha	David Sklansky	$25,500
$1,000 Ace to Five Draw	D Todd	$49,000
$5,000 7-Card Stud	Stu Ungar	$110,000

5-Card Draw was dropped from the WSOP this year.

This was the first year the WSOP had satellite events so players could win full buy-ins. It was the idea of tournament organizer Eric Drache.

Doyle Brunson became the first player to win more than $1,000,000 in WSOP events.

Donnacha O'Dea was the first non-American ever to cash in the WSOP.

1983, April 22nd – The IRS seized $46,000 in poker chips from professional poker player Sarge Ferris while he was playing in a game in Binion's Horseshoe, a Las Vegas poker room.

> *The income tax has made more liars out*
> *of the American people than golf has.*
>
> Will Rogers

1983, May 12 – WSOP Champion Tom McEvoy and runner-up Rod Peate each won their main event seats by winning satellites. They won a combined $756,000 with a combined investment of only $100.

Last year's WSOP Champion, Jack Straus, was knocked out early by Gabe Kaplan. Straus held pocket 9s against Kaplan's KJ. Kaplan got a King on the flop.

Tom McEvoy and Rod Peate played head-up for the title for more than seven hours, a record that stood until 2006.

Benny Binion said that if he ever got a chance to win the country, "I'd close it down and start over."

Doyle Brunson busted out while holding J♦ 9♦. The flop was 7♦ 5♦ 9♣. Rod Peate was holding 9♠ 9♥ and Doyle didn't make his flush.

Minutes after winning the WSOP, Tom McEvoy was asked, 'Does your strategy change when you get to one-on-one?" His answer was, "Yes it does but I don't care to discuss it."

*I truthfully have to say that I'm glad it was me
and Rod and not Doyle Brunson or some of the
other Texans. I got nothing against Texans, but
for years they think they're the best in the world.
I'm from Michigan, Rod's from Washington, and
the Texans have got some competition.*

Tom McEvoy, after winning
the 1983 WSOP main event

Tom McEvoy organized the first non-smoking WSOP tournament and is the driving force behind all other WSOP non-smoking events.

I'm high as a kite right now.

Tom McEvoy
Minutes after winning the 1983 WSOP

1983 – Joe Bernstein was inducted into the Poker Hall of Fame.

1984
15TH WORLD SERIES OF POKER
"Gentleman" Jack Keller

Winner: Jack Keller
Runner-up: Byron "Cowboy" Wolford
# of Players: 132
Prize: $660,000

The Final Hand:

Odds:		Pre-flop/	Flop/	Turn
Keller	T♠ T♥	79.72	78.38	
Board:	5♦ 6♠ 9♣ 8♠ J♦			
Wolford	6♥ 4♥	19.74	21.62	

The final table was:

1st	Jack Keller	$660,000
2nd	Byron Wolford	$264,000
3rd	Jesse Alto	$132,000
4th	David Chew	$66,000
5th	Rick Hamill	$66,000
6th	Curtis Skinner	$52,800
7th	Mike Allen	$26,400
8th	Howard Andrew	$26,400
9th	Rusty LaPage	$26,400

The rest of the WSOP's events winners were:

$1,000 No Limit Hold'em	Dick Albano	$117,000
$1,500 No Limit Hold'em	Todd Baur	$133,500
$1,000 Pot Limit Omaha	William Bennett	$84,000
$1,000 7-Card Stud	Norman Berliner	$50,000
$1,000 Ace to Five Draw	Paul Fontaine	$54,500
$1,000 7-Card Stud	Mike Hart	$40,000

$5,000 7-Card Stud	Jack Keller	$137,000
$1,000 7-Card Stud	John Lucas	$74,000
$1,000 Limit Hold'em	Bob Martinez	$135,000
$1,000 7-Card Stud	Mike Schneiberg	$65,000
$10,000 2-7 Draw	Dewey Tomko	$105,000
$5,000 Pot Limit Omaha	Dewey Tomko	$135,000
$500 Ladies' 7-Card Stud	Karen Wolfson	$15,000

Jack Keller was a former U.S. Air Force pilot.

Jack Keller is the father of professional poker player Kathy Kolberg.

Mike Caro published *Caro's Book of Poker Tells*. It is the first book devoted entirely to the study of poker tells.

> *Players are either acting or they aren't. If they*
> *are acting, decide what they want you to do and*
> *disappoint them.*

Mike Caro's Greatest Law of Tells, 1984

1984 – Bob Stupak defeats a poker-playing Apple II computer with a program called ORAC. Mike Caro wrote the poker program and ORAC is Caro, backwards.

1984 – Pot-Limit Omaha was added to the WSOP tournament schedule.

1984 – Murph Harrold was inducted into the Poker Hall of Fame.

1985
16TH WORLD SERIES OF POKER
Bill Smith

Winner:	Bill Smith
Runner-up:	T. J. Cloutier
# of Players:	140
Prize:	$700,000

The Final Hand:

Odds:		Pre-flop/	Flop/	Turn
Smith	3♠ 3♥	65.33	66.97	70.45

Board: 4♥ 5♠ T♦ 5♣ J♣

Cloutier	A♠ 3♣	32.63	28.59	29.55

The final table was:

1st	Bill Smith	$700,000
2nd	T.J. Cloutier	$280,000
3rd	Berry Johnston	$140,000
4th	Scott Mayfield	$70,000
5th	Hamid Dastmalchi	$70,000
6th	Jesse Alto	$42,000
7th	Johnny Moss	$42,000

The rest of the WSOP's events winners were:

$2,500 Ace to Five Draw	Dick Carson	$50,000
$1,000 Limit Hold'em	Johnny Chan	$171,000
$10,000 2-7 Draw	Tommy Fischer	$95,000
$1,000 No Limit Hold'em	Rich Hamil	$152,000
$1,000 Ace to Five Draw	Mark Mitchell	$63,500
$500 Ladies 7-Card Stud	Rose Pifer	$18,500
$5,000 Pot Limit Omaha	Amarill Slim Preston	$85,000
$1,000 Pot Limit Omaha	Tony Thang	$55,000
$5,000 7-Card Stud	Harry Thomas	$122,500
$1,000 7-Card Stud	Don Williams	$85,000
$1,000 7-Card Razz	Edwin Wyde	$83,000

Cowboy Wolford said of Bill Smith, "If it weren't for the alcohol, he probably would have won three or four world championships instead of just one."

Everyone who knew Bill Smith said that the more he drank, the better he played.

1985 – *The President's Commission on Organized Crime* reported that it considered gambling to be a legitimate industry.

1985 – Actor Telly Savalas of *Kojak* fame placed 3rd in the 7-Card Stud High-Low Split event. He won$14,900 for that win. His lifetime WSOP winnings are $34,600.

1985 – Red Hodges was inducted into the Poker Hall of Fame.

Christ, he's thin. Look at him.
He looks like the advance man for a famine.

Sarge Ferris on Amarillo Slim

1986
17TH WORLD SERIES OF POKER
Berry Johnston

Winner:	Berry Johnston
Runner-up:	Mike Harthcock
# of Players:	141
Prize:	$570,000

The Final Hand:

Odds:		Pre-flop	
Johnston	A♠ T♥	62.14	Tie: 10.08

Board: Unknown

Harthcock	A♦ 8♦	27.77

The final table was:

1st	Berry Johnston	$570,000
2nd	Mike Harthcock	$228,000
3rd	Gary Berland	$114,000

4th	Jesse Alto	$62,000
5th	Bill Smith	$51,300
6th	Roger Moore	$39,000

The rest of the WSOP's winners events were:

$1,000 Limit Omaha	Jim Allen	$48,000
$2,500 Pot Limit Omaha w/rebuys	David Baxter	$127,000
$1,500 No Limit Hold'em	Hamid Dastmalchi	$165,000
$500 Ladies 7-Card Stud	Barbara Enright	$16,400
$5,000 2-7 Draw w/rebuy	Ron Graham	$142,000
$1,500 Limit Hold'em	Jay Heimowitz	$175,800
$1,000 7-Card Razz	Tom McEvoy	$52,400
$1,000 Ace to Five Draw	J.B. Randall	$69,200
$1,000 7-Card Hi-Lo Split	Tommy fischer	$73,600
$1,500 7-Card Stud	Sam Mastrogiannis	$80,000
$5,000 No Limit A-5 Draw w/Joker & R	Mike Cox	$118,000

Berry Johnston said that the title meant more to him than the money.

Before winning the championship this year, Berry Johnston took 3rd place in the main event in 1982.

Berry Johnston holds the record for the most cashes in the WSOP main event at 10.

1983 WSOP Champion Tom McEvoy busted out while holding A♥K♦.

Jesse Alto made the WSOP main event final table a total of six times between 1975 and 1986.

This was the first year that the Joker was used in a WSOP bracelet event.

1986, May 21st – Wendeen Eolis became the first woman to cash in a WSOP main event. She won $10,000 for finishing in 25th place.
1986 – Henry Green was inducted into the Poker Hall of Fame.

1987
18TH WORLD SERIES OF POKER
Johnny "The Orient Express" Chan

Winner: Johnny Chan
Runner-up: Frank Henderson
# of Players: 152
Prize: $655,000

The Final Hand:

Odds:		Pre-flop/	Flop/	Turn
Chan	A♠ 9♣	45.63	28.28	13.64
Board:	5♣ 8♥ K♦ T♣ 9♥			
Henderson	4♦ 4♣	53.88	71.72	86.36

The final table was:

1st	Johnny Chan	$655,000
2nd	Frank Henderson	$250,000
3rd	Bob Ciaffone	$125,000
4th	James Spain	$68,750
5th	Howard Lederer	$56,250
6th	Dan Harrington	$43,750

The rest of the WSOP's events winners were:

$1,000 Ace to Five Draw	Bob Addison	$96,400
$5,000 2-7 Draw w/rebuy	Billy Baxter	$153,000
$1,000 Limit Omaha	T.J. Cloutier	$72,000
$5,000 7-Card Stud	Artie Cobb	$142,000
$1,000 7-Card Stud	Jim Craig	$103,000
$2,500 Pot Limit Omaha	Hal Kant	$174,000
$1,500 Limit Hold'em	Ralph Morton	$189,000
$1,000 7-Card Stud Split	Joe Petro	$93,000
$5,000 7-Card Stud Razz	Carl Rouss	$65,200

| $500 Ladies 7-Card Stud | Linda Ryke-Drucker | $16,800 |
| $1,500 No Limit Hold'em | Hilbert Shirey | $171,600 |

Johnny Chan is the first foreign-born winner of the WSOP. He was born in Guangzhon, China, a city near Hong Kong.

Johnny Chan is a devout non-smoker and non-drinker. His lucky card holder is an orange that he says helps eliminate the cigarette smoke.

After busting out early in the main event, 1982 WSOP Champion Jack Straus said, "I'm going to go to my room and sleep like a baby—sleep an hour, cry an hour, sleep an hour…."

At age 23, Howard Lederer becomes the youngest-yet player to make the final table of the WSOP main event. Finishing in 5th place, he lost to Bob Ciaffone's four 9s.

1983 WSOP Champion Tom McEvoy busted out while holding A♠A♥.

Many WSOP Champions have written poker books. However, *not one* ever wrote his book before he won the championship. The closest anyone has ever come was when 1987 3rd place finisher Bob Ciaffone wrote *Poker Rules* in 1983.

1987 – Walter Clyde "Puggy" Pearson was inducted into the Poker Hall Fame.

1987 – June 26th – 2008 WSOP Champion Peter Eastgate was born.

1987 – California legalized other forms of casino poker besides 5-Card Draw.

1988
19TH WORLD SERIES OF POKER
Johnny "The Orient Express" Chan

Winner: Johnny Chan
Runner-up: Erik Seidel
# of Players: 167
Prize: $700,000

The Final Hand:

Odds:		Pre-flop/	Flop/	Turn
Chan	J♣ 9♣	45.37	96.26	100
Board:	Q♠ T♥ 8♦ 2♠ 6♦			
Seidel	Q♣ 7♠	53.69	2.85	00.00

The final table was:

1st	Johnny Chan	$700,000
2nd	Erik Seidel	$280,000
3rd	Ron Graham	$140,000
4th	Humberto Brenes	$83,050
5th	T.J. Cloutier	$63,000
6th	Jim Bechtel	$49,000

The rest of the WSOP's events winners were:

$1,500 Limit Hold'em	Val Carpenter	$223,800
$1,500 No Limit Hold'em	Russ Gibe	$181,800
$2,500 Pot Limit Omaha	Gilbert Gross	$181,000
$5,000 7-Card Stud	Thor Hansen	$158,000
$1,000 Limit Omaha	David Helms	$91,200
$1,500 7-Card Stud Split	Lance Hilt	$123,600
$500 Ladies 7-Card Stud	Loretta Huber	$17,000
$1,500 7-Card Stud	Merrill Hunt	$130,200
$5,000 2-7 Draw	Seymour Leibowitz	$157,500
$1,500 Ace to 5 Draw	Johnny Moss	$116,400
$1,000 7-Card Razz	Don Williams	$76,800

Johnny Chan won his second consecutive title by flopping a straight against Erik Seidel. The final hand of the WSOP is replayed in the 1998 movie *Rounders*.

The only two-time (or more) winners of the WSOP main event are Johnny Moss, Doyle Brunson, Johnny Chan and Stu Ungar.

This was the first year Phil Hellmuth played in the WSOP main event. He was knocked out in 33rd place by Johnny Chan. The next year, 1989, Phil and Johnny finished 1st and 2nd.

1976 – '77 WSOP Champion Doyle Brunson busted out on Day 1.

1988, August—1982 World Series of Poker Jack Straus died while at the poker table at a game in Los Angeles, California.

1988 – Binion's Horseshoe opened their first poker room after acquiring their next door neighbor, the Mint Casino.

1988 – Doyle Brunson and Jack Straus were inducted into the Poker Hall of Fame.

1988 – Live poker, with a $5 betting limit, was legalized in the historic town of Deadwood, South Dakota.

1988 – In California, Texas Hold'em was declared by the courts to be legally "distinct from Stud-Horse Poker." (Tibbets v. DeCamp, Cal. Reporter 792 (1990))

1988, November 19th—2009 WSOP main event champion Joseph Cada was born.

1989
20TH WORLD SERIES OF POKER
Phil "The Poker Brat" Hellmuth, Jr.

June 11th, 1989
Winner: Phil Hellmuth
Runner-up: Johnny Chan
# of Players: 178
Prize: $755,000

The Final Hand:

Odds:		Pre-flop/	Flop/	Turn
Hellmuth	9♠ 9♣	67.47	73.84	70.45

Board: K♣ T♣ K♦ Q♠ 6♠

Chan   A♠ 7♠   32.10   25.25   29.55

The final table was:

1st	Phil Hellmuth, Jr.	$755,000
2nd	Johnny Chan	$302,000
3rd	Don Zewin	$151,000
4th	Steve Lott	$83,050
5th	Lyle Berman	$67,950
6th	Noel Furlong	452,850

The rest of the WSOP's events winners were:

$1,000 Limit Hold'em	George Allen Shaw	$179,600
$1,500 7-Card Razz	John Laudon	$95,400
$1,500 7-Card Stud Split	Mike Sexton	$104,000
$500 Ladies 7-Card Stud	Alma McClelland	$18,600
$1,500 Ace to Five Draw	Harry Madoff	$119,400
$1,500 Pot Limit Omaha	Barry Blackburn	$108,000
$1,500 7-Card Stud	Mel Judah	$130,000
$5,000 2-7 Draw	Bob Stupak	$139,500
$5,000 7-Card Stud	Don Holt	$154,000
$1,500 Limit Omaha	Lyle Berman	$108,600
$2,500 Pot Limit Omaha	Frank Henderson	$184,000
$2,000 No Limit Hold'em	Norman Keyser	$244,000
$2,000 Limit Hold'em	Thomas Chung	$212,000

At age 24, Phil Hellmuth is the youngest-yet winner of the WSOP.

After winning the WSOP main event the two previous years, Johnny Chan finished second this year.

This was Benny Binion's last WSOP as he passed away on Christmas Day, 1989.
1989 – Fred "Sarge" Ferris was inducted into the Poker Hall of Fame.

1989 – Iowa legalized riverboat casino gambling, with a $5 limit on bets.

1990
21ST WORLD SERIES OF POKER
Mansour Matloubi

Winner: Mansour Matloubi
Runner-up: Hans "Tuna" Lund
# of Players: 194
Prize: $895,000

The Final Hand:

Odds:		Pre-flop/	Flop/	Turn
Matloubi	6♠ 6♥	79.77	87.17	95.45
Board:	8♣ Q♣ 2♥ K♦ 2♣			
Lund	4♦ 4♣	18.33	12.83	4.55

The final table was:

1st	Mansour Matloubi	$895,000
2nd	Hans "Tuna" Lund	$334,000
3rd	Dave Crunkleton	$167,000
4th	Jim Ward	$91,850
5th	Berry Johnston	$75,150
6th	Al Krux	$58,450

The rest of the WSOP's events winners were:

$1,500 Limit Hold'em	Mike Hart	$252,000
$1,500 7-Card Stud	Ray Rumler	$111,600
$1,500 7-Card Stud Split	Norm Boulus	$108,600
$1,500 Omaha 8/B	Monte Kouz	$113,400
$1,500 Limit Omaha	Tony Stormzand	$106,800
$1,500 Ace to Five Draw	Phil Reher	$124,200
$1,500 7-Card Stud	Tai Ta	$158,400
$1,500 Pot Limit Omaha	Shawqui Shunnarah	$113,400
$5,000 2-7 Draw	John Bonetti	$83,250

$5,000 7-Card Stud	Hugh Todd	$168,000
$5,000 Pot Limit Omaha	Amarillo Slim Preston	$142,000
$2,500 Limit Hold'em	Berry Johnston	$254,000
$2,500 No Limit Hold'em	Allen Baker	$280,000
$500 Ladies 7-Card Stud	Marie Gabert	$22,000

This is the first year that Omaha 8/B High-Low was played in the WSOP for a bracelet. It was a $1,500 buy-in event won by Las Vegas professional player Monte Kouz.

Mansour Matloubi is the first non-American citizen to win the WSOP. He was born in Iran and lived in Wales at the time of his win. He now resides in London.

After Mansour Matloubi got head-up with Hans Lund, he went all-in twice while holding a pocket pair. Both times he was losing after the turn and both times he hit his 21-1 longshot on the river to win the hands.

Saying that "….one million dollars is the magic number…" WSOP organizer Jack Binion guarantees a $1,000,000 first prize in next year's WSOP.

At the end of Day 2 of the main event, Stu Ungar had a huge chip lead and was apparently on his way to probably winning the WSOP for a third time. However, he suffered from a drug overdose that night and could not show up to play at all on the third day. His chip lead was so great that even after being blinded off in his absence, he still made the final table on Day 4 and earned $20,500 for finishing in 9th place.

1986 WSOP Champion Berry Johnston took 5th place this year.

Q: What are you going to do with the money?

A: I'm going to keep playing poker.

Mansour Matloubi

1990 – Omaha High-Low Split was added to the WSOP tournament schedule.

1990 – Benny Binion was inducted into the Poker Hall of Fame.

1990, November 6th—Colorado voters approved a constitutional amendment that would allow gambling in Black Hawk, Central City and Cripple Creek.

1991
22ND WORLD SERIES OF POKER
Brad Daugherty

Winner: Brad Daugherty
Runner-up: Don Holt
# of Players: 215
Prize: $1,000,000

The Final Hand:

Odds:		Pre-flop/	Flop/	Turn
Daugherty	K♠ J♠	63.99	77.88	81.82
Board	8♦ 9♥ J♣ 5♣ 8♠			
Holt	7♥ 3♥	62.67	83.23	9.09

The final table was:

1st	Brad Daugherty	$1,000,000
2nd	Don Holt	$402,000
3rd	Bob Veltri	$201,250
4th	Don Williams	$115,000
5th	Perry Green	$69,000
6th	Ali Farsai	$34,500

The rest of the WSOP's events winners were:

$1,500 Omaha 8/B	Joe Becker	$119,400
$2,500 No Limit Hold'em	Doyle Brunson	$208,000
$1,500 No Limit Hold'em	Brent Carter	$166,800
$5,000 7-Card Stud	Thomas Chung	$142,000
$1,500 7-Card Stud	Artie Cobb	$146,400
$1,500 Ace to Five Draw	Pat Flanagan	$106,000
$1,500 7-Card Stud Hi-Low	Mike Harthcock	$106,200
$5,000 Pot Limit Omaha	Jay Heimowitz	$126,000

$1,500 Limit Omaha	Max Lindel	$256,000
$2,500 7-Card Stud	Rodney H. Pardey	$133,000
$5,000 2-7 Draw	John Spadavecchia	$58,500
$2,500 Limit Hold'em	Ron Stanley	$203,000
$1,500 Pot Limit Omaha	An Tran	$87,600
$500 Ladies' 7-Card Stud	Donna Ward	$28,200
$5,000 Limit Hold'em	"Cowboy" Wolford	$210,000
$1,500 7-Card Razz	Charles Wright	$231,000

Brad Daugherty is the first main event champion to win a $1,000,000 first prize.

1973 WSOP Champion Puggy Pearson arrived at this year's WSOP main event dressed to the hilt as an Arab shiek.

Jack Binion predicted that the future growth of the WSOP would be about 10-15% per year.

Brad Daugherty currently lives in the Philippines.

1991 – David Edward "Chip" Reese was inducted into the Poker Hall of Fame.

1991 – Live poker, with a $5 betting limit, was legalized in Colorado.

1991—The state of California repealed the law forbidding the play of Stud Horse Poker, which had been in effect since 1885. Californians could now legally play the game, but there was one problem. No one, not even the Attorney General of the State of California, knew how to play the game!

1992
23RD WORLD SERIES OF POKER
Hamid Dastmalchi

Winner: Hamid Dastmalchi
Runner-up: Tom Jacobs
# of Players: 201
Prize: $1,000,000

The Final Hand:

Odds:		Pre-flop/	Flop/	Turn
Dastmalchi	8♥ 4♣	36.04	16.77	90.91

Board: J♥ 5♦ 7♦ 6♥ 8♣

Jacobs	J♦ 7♠	62.67	83.23	9.09

The final table was:

1st	Hamid Dastmalchi	$1,000,000
2nd	Tom Jacobs	$353,500
3rd	Hans "Tuna" Lund	$176,750
4th	Mike Alsaadi	$101,000
5th	Dave Crunkleton	$60,600
6th	Clyde Coleman	$30,300

The rest of the WSOP's events winners were:

$1,500 7-Card Stud	Men Nguyen	$120,000
$1,500 Pot Limit Hold'em	Buddy Bonnecaze	$115,800
$1,500 7-Card Razz	Lamar Hampton	$80,400
$1,500 Omaha 8/B	Eli Balas	$122,400
$1,500 No Limit Hold'em	Lance Straughn	$152,400
$1,500 7-Card Stud Split	Rick Steiner	$105,000
$1,500 Limit Hold'em	Bob Abell	$226,800
$1,500 Limit Omaha	Tom McEvoy	$79,200
$1,500 Pot Limit Omaha	Billy Thomas	$81,000
$5,000 2-7 Draw	Mickey Appleman	$119,250
$1,500 Ace to Five Draw	Dal Derovin	$90,000
$1,500 Limit Hold'em	Erik Seidel	$168,000
$2,500 7-Card Stud	Ray Rumler	$106,000
$5,000 Pot Limit Omaha	Hoyt Corkins	$96,000
$2,500 Pot Limit Hold'em	Kenny Duggan	$134,000
$5,000 7-Card Stud	Paul "Eskimo" Clark	$122,000
$2,500 No Limit Hold'em	Lyle Berman	$192,000
$5,000 Limit Hold'em	Phil Hellmuth	$168,00
$1,000 Ladies' 7-Card Stud	Shari Flanzer	$38,000

Hamid Dastmalchi is the second Iranian-born winner of the WSOP.

After the flop, Dastmalchi had a gut shot straight draw while Jacobs had flopped two pair—Jack and 7s. Jacobs bet $30,000 into at $40,000 pot. Dastmalchi called and caught the 6♥ to make his straight. He then won the championship when Jacobs didn't get a Jack or a 7 on the river to make a full house. After the tournament, Dastmalchi said, "He didn't make enough bet—let me stay to catch the card that break him. He make a mistake."

The number of entrants in the WSOP main event has increased every year since the inaugural year of 1970, until this year. Entries were down to 201 in 1992, down from a high of 215 in 1991.

Former champions Johnny Chan and Jack Keller each almost made the final table this year.

1992 – Thomas "Amarillo Slim" Preston was inducted into the Poker Hall of Fame.

1992 – March 10th – Harrison County, Mississippi votes to legalize casino-style riverboat gambling.

1992, August – The first hand of legal poker dealt in Mississippi was won by poker writer Ken Warren. That landmark hand was a Texas Hold'em hand of 7s full of Kings while holding K♥7♥ in the big blind at the President Casino.

1992 – The U.S. Congress legalized gambling on U.S. flagships.

1992 – The first Shuffle Master Model BG-1, a machine that could shuffle and count the deck in 45 seconds, was introduced in Las Vegas. It was conceived and built by truck driver John Breeding.

1992, November 3rd—Missouri voters approved, by a margin of 63% to 37%, a referendum that allows gambling boat excursions on the Mississippi and Missouri Rivers. There is a loss limit of $500 per person per excursion.

1993
24TH WORLD SERIES OF POKER
Jim Bechtel

Winner: Jim Bechtel
Runner-up: Glen Cozen
# of Players: 220
Prize: $1,000,000

The Final Hand:

Odds:		Pre-flop/	Flop/	Turn
Bechtel	J♣ 6♥	60.71	75.15	86.36
Board:	T♦ 8♠ 3♣ 2♣ 5♦			
Cozen	7♠ 4♦	38.00	24.85	13.64

The final table was:

1st	Jim Bechtel	$1,000,000
2nd	Glenn Cozen	$420,000
3rd	John Bonetti	$210,000
4th	Mansour Matloubi	$120,000
5th	Thomas Chung	$72,000
6th	Mike Cowley	$36,000

The rest of the WSOP's events winners were:

$,1500 Limit Hold'em	Hugo Meith	$220,800
$1,500 7-Card Stud	Robert Turner	$103,800
$1,500 Limit Omaha	Jack Keller	$61,800
$1,500 7-Card Stud	Gene Fisher	$113,400
$1,500 7-Card Razz	Ted Forrest	$77,400
$1,500 Omaha 8/B	Ted Forrest	$120,000
$1,500 No Limit Hold'em	Phil Hellmuth	$161,400
$1,500 Pot Limit Omaha	Daniel Trujillo	$83,000
$5,000 2-7 Draw	Billy Baxter	$130,000

$1,500 Ace to Five Draw	Chau Giang	$82,800
$2,500 Pot Limit Hold'em	Hamid Dastmalchi	$114,000
$2,500 7-Card Stud	Marty Sigel	$113,000
$1,500 Pot Limit Omaha	Humberto Brenes	$73,600
$2,500 Limit Omaha	Humberto Brenes	$149,000
$5,000 7-Card Stud	Ted Forrest	$114,000
$2,5000 No Limit Hold'em	Phil Hellmuth	$173,000
$5,000 Limit Hold'em	Phil Hellmuth	$138,000
$1,000 Ladies 7-Card Stud	Phyllis Kessler	$32,800

Jim Bechtel's winning hand was only a Jack-high—the lowest poker hand to ever win the WSOP main event. That record still stands as of 2008.

After Hal Fowler, Jim Bechtel is only the second amateur to win the WSOP.

After only the third hand after the action got head-up, Jim Bechtel called an all-in bet from Glen Cozen without looking at his cards. He had only J♣6♥ but he won the hand, and the title, anyway.

1990 WSOP Champion Mansour Matloubi placed 4th in the main event, winning $120,000.

Jim Bechtel currently resides in Gilbert, Arizona.

> *In the tournament I won at Caesar's Palace a*
> *few years ago I had one chip left at one point*
> *and I won the tournament. I've learned that*
> *you're never out of it*

> Glen Cozen, 1993

1993 – 1984 WSOP Champion Jack Keller was inducted into the Poker Hall of Fame.

1994
25TH WORLD SERIES OF POKER
Russ Hamilton

Winner: Russ Hamilton
Runner-up: Hugh Vincent
# of Players: 268
Prize: $1,000,000 plus his weight in gold, which came to $28,512 (330 pounds @ $5.40 per ounce). That's also after they confiscated more than 100 pounds of nickels he had stuffed in his pockets.

The Final Hand:

Odds:		Pre-flop/	Flop/	Turn
Hamilton	K♠ 8♥	70.71	81.52	93.18

Board: 8♠ 2♠ 6♦ T♣ J♠

Vincent	8♣ 5♥	25.72	14.95	6.82

The final table was:

1st	Russ Hamilton	$1,000,000 + his weight in silver
2nd	Hugh Vincent	$588,000
3rd	John Spadavecchia	$294,000
4th	Vince Burgio	$168,000
5th	Al Krux	$100,800
6th	Robert Turner	$50,400

The rest of the WSOP's events winners were:

$1,500 Limit Hold'em	Steven Sim	$289,200
$1,500 7-Card Stud	Johnny Chan	$135,600
$1,500 Limit Omaha	Brent Carter	$83,400
$1,500 7-Card Stud Split	Vince Burgio	$127,200
$1,500 7-Card Razz	Mike Hart	$88,800
$1,500 Omaha 8/B	T.J. Cloutier	$135,000

$1,500 No Limit Hold'em	George Rodis	$135,000
$1,500 Pot Limit Omaha	O'Neil Longson	$100,800
$1,500 Pot Limit Hold'em	Jay Heimiwitz	$148,200
$2,500 Omaha 8/B	J.C. Pearson	$103,000
$5,000 NL 2-7 Draw	Lyle Berman	$128,250
$1,500 Ace to Five Draw	J.J. Chun	$93,000
$2,500 Limit Hold'em	Mike Laving	$212,000
$2,500 7-Card Stud	Rodney H. Pardey	$132,000
$2,500 Pot Limit Omaha	Huck Seek	$167,000
$5,000 7-Card Stud	Roger Moore	$144,000
$2,500 No Limit Hold'em	John Heaney	$220,000
$5,000 Limit Hold'em	Erik Seidel	$210,000
$1,000 Ladies' 7-Card Stud	Barbara Enright	$38,400
Press Invitational No Limit Hold'em	Bill Sykes	$1,000

This year was the silver anniversary of the WSOP. In commemoration, the winner was awarded his weight in silver.

After the flop of what turned out to be the final hand, Russ Hamilton said, "I'm going all-in." Hugh Vincent said, "I call," but his remark was almost unintelligible because he was talking with a mouthful of a huge hamburger.

Russ Hamilton made the first King-high straight flush in any main event while holding K♣ J♣.

1994 – The first on-line operational casino was created by Mircogaming, an on-line casino software supplier.

1995
26TH WORLD SERIES OF POKER
"Action" Dan Harrington

Winner: Dan Harrington
Runner-up: Howard Goldfarb
# of Players: 273
Prize: $1,000,000

The Final Hand:

Odds:		Pre-flop/	Flop/	Turn
Harrington	9♦ 8♦	46.88	85.15	93.18

Board: 8♣ 2♥ 6♦ Q♠ Q♥

Goldfarb	A♥ 7♣	52.75	14.85	6.82

The final table was:

1st	Dan Harrington	$1,000,000
2nd	Howard Goldfarb	$519,000
3rd	Brent Carter	$302,250
4th	Hamid Dastmalchi	$173,000
5th	Barbara Enright	$114,180
6th	Chuck Thompson	$86,500

The rest of the WSOP's events winners were:

$1,500 Limit Hold'em	Christian Van Hees	$315,000
$1,500 7-Card Stud	Valter Farina	$144,600
$1,500 Limit Omaha	Berry Johnston	$91,200
$1,500 Chinese Poker	John Tsagaris	$41,400
$1,500 7-Card Stud Split	Rod Peate	$127,200
$1,500 7-Card Razz	Mickey Sisskind	$82,800
$1,500 Omaha 8/B	Max Stern	$140,000
$1,500 No Limit Hold'em	Richard Klaiman	$205,875
$1,500 Pot Limit Omaha	Phil "Doc" Earle	$143,000
$1,500 Pot Limit Hold'em	Peter Vilandos	$148,500
$5,000 2-7 Draw	John Bonetti	$101,250
$2,500 7-Card Stud Split	Men Nguyen	$96,000
$2,500 Omaha 8/B	Marlon De Los Santos	$119,000
$1,500 Ace to Five Draw	Clifford Roof	$81,600
$5,000 Chinese Poker	Steve Zolotow	$112,500
$2,500 Limit Hold'em	Men Nyugen	$186,000
$2,500 7-Card Stud	Dan Robison	$140,000
$2,500 Pot Limit Omaha	Hilbert Shirey	$137,000
$2,500 Pot Limit Hold'em	Hilbert Shirey	$163,000

$5,000 7-Card Stud	Anthony DeAngelo	$130,000
$2,500 No Limit Hold'em	Dan Harrington	$249,000
$5,000 Limit Hold'em	Mickey Appleman	$234,000
$1,000 Ladie's 7-Card Stud	Starla Brodie	$35,200

Johnny Moss has played in every WSOP from 1970 to 1995. This was his last one, as he passed away later this year.

Barbara Enright became the first, and as of 2009, the only woman to make it to the final table at the WSOP main event. She busted out in 5th place while holding pocket 8s. She raised preflop and was called by Brent Carter who was holding a lowly 6♠ 4♣. The flop was T♦ 6♥ 4♠ and when the board didn't improve on the turn or river, she threw her cards down on the table in disgust and picked up her $114,000 win.

Dan Harrington won the 1971 Massachusetts State Chess Championship.

Dan Harrington is cousin to pro golfer Padraig Harrington and NFL quarterback Joey Harrington.

1992 WSOP Champion Hamid Dastmalchi finished in 4th place this year, earning $173,000.

The flop for the final hand dealt in both the 1994 and 1995 WSOP main events were both 826—8♦ 2♠ 6♦ in 1994 and 8♣ 2♥ 6♦ in 1995.

Dan Harrington always wears a green Boston Red Sox baseball cap when playing poker.

Dan Harrington currently resides in Santa Monica, California.

1995, February 18th – "C-Day." Mike Caro simultaneously introduces his new four-color deck of cards at 65 worldwide casino poker rooms.

The colors were:

♠ - traditional black
♥ - traditional red
♣ - green
♦ - blue

Beginners and novices were quite accepting of the new colors while veteran players rejected it with a "…you gotta be kidding me," stunned silence. It was a failure.

1995, June—A new television game show featuring real strip poker was reviewed by the USA Network. It failed because, as one viewer said, "Because this is American cable TV, viewers never actually see any nudity."

1995, December 16th – 1970, '71, and '74 World Series of Poker Champion Johnny Moss died at age 88.

1996
27TH WORLD SERIES OF POKER
Huckleberry "Huck" Seed

Winner: Huck Seed
Runner-up: Dr. Bruce Van Horn
# of Players: 295
Prize: $1,000,000

The Final Hand:

Odds:		Pre-flop/	Flop/	Turn
Seed	9♦ 8♦	31.74	83.94	93.18
Board:	9♥ 8♥ 4♥ A♥ 3♠			
Van Horn	K♣ 8♣	65.51	16.06	6.82

The final table was:

1st	Huck Seed	$1,000,000
2nd	Dr. Bruce Van Horn	$585,000
3rd	John Bonetti	$341,250
4th	Men Nguyen	$195,000
5th	An Tran	$128,700
6th	Andre Boyer	$97,500

The rest of the WSOP's events winners were:

$1,500 Chinese Poker	Gregory Grival	$37,200
$2,000 Limit Hold'em	David Chiu	$396,000
$1,500 7-Card Stud	Gary Benson	$148,200
$1,500 Limit Omaha	Dudy Roach	$102,600
$1,500 7-Card Stud Split	John Cernuto	$147,000
$1,500 7-Card Razz	Randy Holland	$87,000
$1,500 Omaha 8/B	Adeeb Harb	$155,815
$41,500 No Limit Hold'em	John Morgan	$227,815
$1,500 Pot Limit Omaha	Jim Huntley	$168,600
$1,500 Pot Limit Hold'em	Al Krux	$156,375
$5,000 2-7 Draw	Freddy Deeb	$146,250
$2,500 7-Card Stud Split	Frank Thompson	$94,000
$2,500 Omaha 8/B	Men Nguyen	$110,000
$5,000 Chinese Poker	Jim Fieldhouse	$50,000
$1,500 Ace to Five Draw	Hans "Tuna" Lund	$71,400
$3,000 Limit Hold'em	Donny Kerr	$200,400
$2,500 7-Card Stud	Marry Sigel	$144,000
$2,500 Pot Limit Omaha	Sammy Farha	$145,000
$2,500 Pot Limit Hold'em	Barbara Enright	$180,000
$5,000 7-Card Stud	Henry Orenstein	$130,000
$$2,500 No Limit Hold'em	Mel Weiner	$250,315
$5,000 Limit Hold'em	Tony Ma	$236,000
$1,000 Ladies' 7-Card Stud	Susie Isaacs	$42,000

Huck Seed was a member of the 1978 Montana All-State Basketball team.

At 6"7", Huck is the tallest-yet winner of the WSOP main event.

At age 27, Huck became the second-youngest yet winner of the WSOP.

This was the last WSOP main event to not be filmed as it happened.

> *I haven't played with many women who are really good*
> *at what they do. They want to invade what they think*
> *is a man's world; it's almost a personal thing, they*
> *want to beat men. I don't understand it. This is*
> *a game of talent. If you have the talent, it's*

not going to matter who you are.

Cissy Bottoms, 1996

1996 – Julius "Little Man" Popwell was inducted into the Poker Hall of Fame.

1996—The United States Poker Championship held their first tournament at the Trump Taj Mahal in Atlantic City, New Jersey. The winner was Ken Flaton.

1997
28TH WORLD SERIES OF POKER
Stuart "Stuey, The Kid" Ungar

Winner: Stu Ungar
Runner-up: John Strzemp
# of Players: 312
Prize: $1,000,000

The Final Hand:

Odds:		Pre-flop/	Flop/	Turn
Ungar	A♥ 4♣	23.98	27.58	15.91
Board	A♣ 5♦ 3♥ 3♦ 2♠			
Strzemp	A♠ 8♣	54.73	57.88	31.82

The final table was:

1st	Stu Ungar	$1,000,000
2nd	John Strzemp	$583,000
3rd	Mel Judah	$371,000
4th	Ron Stanley	$212,000
5th	Bob Walker	$161,120
6th	Peter Bao	$127,200

This was the first year that 6th place paid more than $100,000.

The rest of the WSOP's events winners were:

$2,000 Limit Hold'em	Kevin Song	$397,120
$1,500 7-Card Razz	Linda Johnson	$96,000
$1,500 Limit Omaha	Claude Cohen	$110,400
$1,500 7-Card Stud	Maria Stern	$140,708
$1,500 Pot Limit Omaha	Chris Bjorin	$154,800
$1,500 7-Card Stud Split	Doug Saab	$130,305
$2,000 No Limit Hold'em	John Cernuto	$259,150
$2,000 Omaha 8/B	Scotty Nguyen	$156,950
$2,000 Pot Limit Hold'em	Dave Ulliott	$180,310
$2,500 7-Card Stud	Vasilis Lazarou	$169,000
$2,500 Pot Limit Omaha	Mattias Rochnacher	$183,000
$2,500 7-Card Stud Split	Max Stern	$117,000
$3,000 Limit Hold'em	Louis Asmo	$231,600
$3,000 Omaha 8/B	Dean Stonier	$145,200
$3,000 Pot Limit Hold'em	Phil Hellmuth	$204,000
$5,000 2-7 Draw	Johnny Chan	$164,250
$3,000 No Limit Hold'em	Max Stern	$237,615
$5,000 7-Card Stud	Mel Judah	$176,000
$5,000 Limit Hold'em	Bob Veltri	$224,000
$1,000 Ladies' 7-Card Stud	Susie Issacs	$38,000

Stu Ungar was penniless minutes before the start of the 1997 WSOP main event. Billy Baxter loaned him the buy-in and Stu was the very last player to enter the tournament.

This year's WSOP was kicked off by comedian-actor Milton Berle, who announced, "Players, get ready. Shuffle up and deal."

This was Stu Ungar's third WSOP main event title, tying him with Johnny Moss for the most titles. However, Stu's wins are universally considered to be the greater accomplishment. Johnny Moss defeated a total of only 57 other players and one of his wins was awarded by a vote. Stu Ungar defeated a total of 457 other players in his three wins.

Actor Richard Moll from the television show *Night Court* played in the main event under the name "Pasadena Dick."

Poker book author Steward Reuben won the Press Invitational Tournament.

Stu Ungar wore his trademark blue glasses to hide the fact that his nostrils had collapsed due to years' of drug abuse.

1985 World Series of Poker Champion Bill Smith died.

1997 – Roger Moore was inducted into the Poker Hall of Fame.

1997 – Maria Stern won the WSOP 7-Card Stud event while Max Stern won the 7-Card Stud High-Low event. They were the first husband and wife to win WSOP titles.

1997 – The 'hole cam' was introduced in Europe. It was first used in the "Late Night Poker" Series. The hole camera was invented by Henry Orenstein, and has U.S. Patent # 5,451,054. It's estimated that the creation of the hole cam has facilitated the creation of as many as 150,000 jobs.

1998
29TH WORLD SERIES OF POKER
Thuan "Scotty" Nguyen

Winner: Scotty Nguyen
Runner-up: Kevin McBride
# of Players: 350
Prize: $1,000,000

The Final Hand:

Odds:		Pre-flop/	Flop/	Turn
Nguyen	J♦ 9♣	33.56	94.85	97.73
Board:	8♣ 9♦ 9♥ 8♥ 8♠			
McBride	Q♥ T♥	65.57	5.15	2.27

The final table was:

1st	Scotty Nguyen	$1,000,000
2nd	Kevin McBride	$687,500
3rd	T.J. Cloutier	$437,000
4th	Dewey Weum	$250,000
5th	Lee Salem	$190,000

This was the only year when the final table began with just five players. Scotty Nguyen eliminated two players in one hand right before the two final tables were consolidated.

The rest of the WSOP's events winners were:

$2,000 Limit Hold'em	Farzad Bonyadi	$429,940
$1,500 7-Card Stud	Doyle Brunson	$93,000
$1,500 Limit Omaha	Michael Shadkin	$109,800
$1,500 7-Card Stud	Kirk Morrison	$148,185
$1,500 Pot Limit Omaha	Donnacha O'Dea	$154,800
$1,500 7-Card Stud Split	Tommy Hufnagle	$139,305
$2,000 No Limit Hold'em	Jeff Ross	$259,000
$2,000 Omaha 8/B	Chau Giang	$150,960
$2,000 Pot Limit Hold'em	Daniel Negreanu	$169,460
$2,500 7-Card Stud	Artie Cobb	$152,000
$2,500 Pot Limit Omaha	T.J. Cloutier	$136,000
$2,500 7-Card Stud Split	Bill Gempel	$120,000
$3,000 Limit Hold'em	David Chiu	$205,000
$3,000 Omaha 8/B	Raul Rowe	$133,200
$3,000 Pot Limit Hold'em	Steve Rydel	$206,400
$5,000 Deuce to Seven Draw	Erik Seidel	$132,750
$3,000 No Limit Hold'em	Ken Buntjer	$268,620
$5,000 7-Card Stud	Jan Chen	$208,000
$5,000 Limit Hold'em	Patrick Bruel	$224,000
$1,000 Ladies' 7-Card Stud	Mandy Commanda	$40,000

The $1,000,000 first-prize money was brought to the final table in a cardboard Chiffon toilet paper box.

After the river card, Scotty Nguyen made a bet that would put McBride all-in if he calls. Scotty had a full house of 9s full of 8s while McBride would have to play the 8s full of 9s full house that was on the board. While waiting for McBride to make a decision, Scotty said, "You call, it's gonna be all over, baby." McBride called and lost.

This was Vince Van Patten's first year as a WSOP commentator.

Actors Matt Damon and Ed Norton, the stars of *Rounders,* played in this year's WSOP. Matt Damon was knocked out while holding K♥K♠ by Doyle Brunson, who was holding A♣A♦.

T.J. Cloutier is a former professional football player. He was a tight end for five years in the Canadian Football League.

Kevin McBride, this year's runner-up, was knocked out of an earlier satellite for this tournament by Vince Van Patten. He had to rebuy in a subsequent tournament and fortunately for him, he won that tournament.

Stu Ungar said his reason for not playing in this year's WSOP was, "Showing up in my condition would be more embarrassing than not showing up at all."

Scotty Nguyen does not wear his WSOP bracelet. It's his way of honoring his brother, who was killed in a car accident in Vietnam the day after he won the bracelet.

1998 – This was the first year a player from Canada won a WSOP bracelet. Daniel Negreanu and Mandy Commanda are both from Ontario, Canada.

1998 – Planet Poker became the first on-line poker room.

1998 – Casino owners in Nevada spent over $26,000,000 trying to defeat a referendum in neighboring California that would allow American Indian tribes to open their own casinos. The referendum passed.

1998, November 22nd – 1980, '81, and '97 World Series of Poker Champion Stu Ungar died in Room 16 of the Oasis Motel in downtown Las Vegas, Nevada. Casino owner Bob Stupak took up a collection to cover the costs of Stu's funeral.

1999
30TH WORLD SERIES OF POKER
J. J. "Noel" Furlong

Winner:	Noel Furlong
Runner-up:	Alan Goehring
# of Players:	393
Prize:	$1,000,000

The Final Hand:

Odds:		Pre-flop/	Flop/	Turn
Furlong	5♣ 5♦	17.67	83.23	90.91
Board:	Q♠ Q♣ 5♠ 2♠ 8♠			
Goehring	6♥ 6♣	80.39	16.77	9.09

The final table was:

1st	J.J. "Noel" Furlong	$1,000,000
2nd	Alan Goehring	$768,625
3rd	Padraig Parkinson	$489,125
4th	Erik Seidel	$279,500
5th	Chris Bigler	$212,420
6th	Huck Seed	$167,700

The rest of the WSOP's events winners were:

$1,500 Limit Hold'em	Charles Brahmi	$338,000
$1,500 7-Card Razz	Paul "Eskimo" Clark	$84,610
$2,500 Limit Hold'em	John Esposito	$219,225
$2,500 7-Card Stud	David Grey	$199,000
$2,500 Pot Limit Omaha	Hassan Komoei	$173,000
$2,500 7-Card Stud Hi-	Ron Long	$170,000
$2,500 No Limit Hold'em	Eric Holum	$283,975
$2,500 Limit Omaha	Tom Franklin	$104,000
$2,500 Omaha 8/B	Steve Badger	$186,000

$3,000 Limit Hold'em	Josh Arieh	$202,800
$3,500 No Limit Hold'em	Mike Matusow	$147,000
$3,000 Pot Limit Hold'em	Layne Flack	$224,400
$5,000 Limit Hold'em	Eli Balas	$220,000
$1,000 Ladies' 7-Card Stud	Christina Pie	$34,000
$1,500 Omaha 8/B	Mike Wattel	$134,865

Noel Furlong got his nickname because he was born on Christmas Day.

At age 61, Noel Furlong was the second-oldest player to win the WSOP main event. There's a three-way tie for first place, all held by Johnny Moss!

Noel Furlong, an Irish businessman, became only the second non-American to win the title.

Noel Furlong doesn't play much poker these days because his carpet manufacturing business does more than $100,000,000 in business each year.

1999 – The WSOP had 3,456 total players in all events and paid out $11,291,000 in prize money. By comparison, the 2006 main event winner won $12,000,000 alone.

1999 – The first U.S. poker production funded entirely by a television network rather than a casino was a documentary of the WSOP produced and directed by Steve Lipscomb.

2000
31ST WORLD SERIES OF POKER
Christopher "Jesus" Ferguson

Winner: Chris "Jesus" Ferguson
Runner-up: T. J. Cloutier
# of Players: 512
Prize: $1,500,000

The Final Hand:

Odds:		Pre-flop/	Flop/	Turn
Ferguson	A♠ 9♣	23.09	83.23	90.91
Board:	2♥ K♣ 4♥ K♥ 9♥			
Cloutier	A♦ Q♣	71.05	81.72	79.55

The final table was:

1st	Chris Ferguson	$1,500,000
2nd	T.J. Cloutier	$896,500
3rd	Steve Kaufman	$570,500
4th	Hasan Habib	$326,000
5th	James McManus	$427,760
6th	Roman Abinsay	$195,600

The rest of the WSOP's events winners were:

$500 Casino Employees Limit Hold'em	Dave Alizadeh	$21,800
$2,000 Limit Hold'em	Tony Ma	$367,040
$1,500 7-Card Stud	Jerri Thomas	$135,825
$1,500 Limit Omaha	Ivo Donev	$85,800
$1,500 7-Card Stud Hi-Low	Randy Holland	$120,990
$1,500 Pot Limit Omaha	Johnny Chan	$179,400
$1,500 Limit Omaha Hi-Low	Not Koe	$160,950
$2,000 No Limit Hold'em	Diego Cordovez	$293,040
$2,500 7-Card Stud	Chris Ferguson	$151,000
$2,000 Pot Limit Hold'em	Jimmy Athanas	$173,900
$3,000 Limit Hold'em	Chris Tsiprailidis	$213,600
$5,000 No Limit Deuce to Seven Draw	Jennifer Harman	$146,250
$2,500 7-Card Stud Hi-Low	Joe Wynn	$129,000
$2,500 Pot Limit Omaha	Phil Ivey	$195,000
$1,500 Ace to Five Lowball	Richard Dunberg	$76,200
$2,500 Limit Omaha Hi-Low	Michael Sohayegh	$160,000
$1,500 Razz	Huck Seed	Huck Seed
$3,000 Pot Limit Hold'em	Mike Carson	$222,000
$5,000 7-Card Stud	David Chiu	$202,000

$3,000 No Limit Hold'em	Chris Bjorin	$334,110
$5,000 Limit Omaha Hi-Low	Howard Lederer	$198,000
$5,000 Limit Hold'em	Jay Heimowitz	$284,000
$1,000 ½ Limit Hold'em,	Nani Dollison	$53,200
½ 7-Card Stud Ladies' Championship		
Charity Media Event	Tim Ellis	$5,000

T.J. Cloutier captured 2nd place in the WSOP—for the second time.

Chris Ferguson can throw a playing card 78 mph and can toss a playing card into a hat from 50 feet away. He can also throw a card hard and fast enough to cut a peeled banana in half.

Both of Chris Ferguson's parents hold Ph.D.s in Mathematics and Chris himself has a Ph.D. in Computer Science focusing on "virtual network algorithms."

Although Chris allows others to call him Jesus, he is an atheist.

Kathy Liebert finished 17th in the main event and Annie Duke finished 10th. When it became apparent that either one of these women could possibly win the championship, Amarillo Slim Preston posed behind each one of them while holding a knife to his throat.

Computers are useless.
They can only give you answers.

Pablo Picasso

2000 – Phil Ivey becomes the second African-American to win a WSOP title. He won $195,000 in the $2,500 buy-in Pot Limit Omaha event.

2000, May 5th – Jennifer Harman became the first female to win a WSOP no-limit event. She won $146,000 in the $5,000 buy-in No-Limit Deuce to Seven Stud.
2000 – 1979 WSOP Champion Hal Fowler died.

2000 – Harry and Jerri Thomas of Hamilton, Ohio became the second husband and wife to win WSOP bracelets. Harry won the $5,000 buy-in 7-Card Stud event in 1985 and Jerri won the $1,500 buy-in 7-Card Stud event this year.

2000- *Hustler Magazine* publisher Larry Flynt opened the Hustler Casino on the site of the old El Dorado Casino in Gardena, California.

2000, May – The first on-line poker scandal occurred. An on-line poker room site called Poker Spot owned by popular poker player Dutch Boyd had to close because it could not collect credit card deposits made by players. Unable to pay their players, they had to shut down.

2000 – The Poker Million Tournament boasted the first 1,000,000 pound poker game on live television.

2000 – The betting limit in South Dakota poker rooms is legally raised from $5 to $100.

2000, November—The first Poker Million tournament was held on the Isle of Man. Thirty million worldwide viewers watched John Duthie win the tournament.

2001
32ND WORLD SERIES OF POKER
Juan Carlos "El Matador" Mortensen

Winner: Carlos Mortensen
Runner-up: Dewey Tomko
# of Players: 613
Prize: $1,500,000

The Final Hand:

Odds:		Pre-flop/	Flop/	Turn
Mortensen	K♣ Q♣	17.50	48.48	25.00
Board:	J♦ T♣ 3♣ 3♦ 9♦			
Tomko	A♠ A♥	82.13	51.52	75.00

The final table was:

1st	Juan Carlos Mortensen	$1,500,000
2nd	Dewey Tomko	$1,098,925
3rd	Stan Schrier	$699,315
4th	Phil Gordon	$399,610
5th	Phil Hellmuth, Jr.	$303,705
6th	Mike Matusow	$239,765
7th	Henry Nowakowski	$179,825
8th	Steve Riehle	$119,885
9th	John Inashima	$91,190

This was the first year that a 2nd place finisher won more than $1,000,000.

This was the first year that the final table was expanded to nine players.

The rest of the WSOP's events winners were:

$500 Casino Employees Limit Hold'em	Travis Jonas	$40,200
$2,000 Limit Hold'em	Nani Dollison	$441,440
$1,500 Omaha Hi-Low 8/B	Chris Ferguson	$164,735
$1,500 7-Card Stud	Adam Roberts	$146,430
$2,000 No Limit Hold'em	Phil Hellmuth	$316,550
$1,500 Limit Omaha	Eddy Scharf	$83,810
$1,500 7-Card Stud Hi-Low 8/B	Barry Shulman	$123,820
$1,500 Pot Limit Omaha	Galen Kester	$167,035
$2,000 S.H.O.E.	David Pham	$140,455
$3,000 Limit Hold'em	Jim Lester	$233,490
$2,500 7-Card Stud	Paul Darden	$147,440
$2,000 Pot Limit Hold'em	Burt Boutin	$193,800
$1,500 Razz	Berry Johnston	$83,810
$2,500 Pot Limit Omaha	Scotty Nguyen	$178,480
$2,500 7-Card Stud Hi-Low 8/B	Rich Korbin	$159,080
$1,500 Ace to Five Draw Lowball	Cliff Yamagawa	$73,915
$2,500 Omaha Hi-Low 8/B	Bob Slezak	$173,625
$5,000 2-7 Draw	Howard Lederer	$165,870
$1,000 Seniors' Championship	Jay Heimowitz	$115,430
$3,000 Pot Limit Hold'em	Steve Zolotow	$243,335
$5,000 7-Card Stud	Allen Cunningham	$201,760
$3,000 No Limit Hold'em	Erik Seidel	$411,300

$5,000 Omaha Hi-Low 8/B	Scotty Nguyen	$207,580
$5,000 Limit Hold'em	Hemish Shah	$312,340
$1,000 Ladies' World Championship	Nani Dollison	$41,130

As of 2009, Carlos Mortensen is generally considered to be the last professional poker player to win the WSOP.

Dewey Tomko finished second in this year's WSOP main event—again.

2001 – Stu Ungar was inducted into the Poker Hall of Fame.

2001—The World Heads-Up Poker Championship held their first tournament. The winner was Bruno Fitoussi.

2002
33RD WORLD SERIES OF POKER
Robert Varkonyi

Winner: Robert Varkonyi
Runner-up: Julian Gardner
# of Players: 631
Prize: $2,000,000

The Final Hand:

Odds:		Pre-flop/	Flop/	Turn
Varkonyi	Q♦ T♠	60.40	66.16	75.00
Board:	Q♣ 4♣ 4♠ T♦ T♣			
Gardner	J♣ 8♣	38.73	33.74	25.00

The final table was

1st	Robert Varkonyi	$2,000,000
2nd	Julian Gardner	$1,100,000
3rd	Ralph Perry	$550,000

4th	Scott Gray	$281,480
5th	Harley Hall	$195,000
6th	Russell Rosenblum	$150,000
7th	John Shipley	$125,000
8th	Tony D	$100,000
9th	Minh Ly	$85,000

The rest of the WSOP's events winners were:

$500 Casino Employees Limit Hold'em	David Warga	$47,300
$2,000 Limit Hold'em	Mike Majerus	$407,120
$1,500 Omaha Hi-Low Split	Perry Friedman	$176,860
$2,000 No Limit Hold'em	Layne Flack	$303,880
$1,500 7-Card Stud	Phil Ivey	$132,000
$1,500 Limit Hold'em	John Cernuto	$73,320
$1,500 7-Card Stud Hi-Low Split	Paul Clark	$125,200
$1,500 Pot Limit Omaha	Jack Duncan	$192,560
$2,500 No Limit Hold'em Gold Bracelet Match Play	Johnny Chan	$34,000
$2,000 H.O.R.S.E.	John Hennigan	$117,320
$2,000 Pot Limit Hold'em	Jay Sipelstein	$150,240
$2,500 7-Card Stud	Dan Torla	$115,600
$3,000 Limit Hold'em	John Hom	$174,840
$1,500 Razz	Billy Baxter	$64,860
$2,500 Pot Limit Omaha	Jan Vang Sorensen	$185,000
$2,500 7-Card Stud Hi-Low Split	Phil Ivey	$118,440
$3,000 Pot Limit Hold'em	Fred Berger	$197,400
$1,500 Ace to Five Lowball	Thor Hansen	$62,600
$1,500 No Limit Hold'em	Layne Flack	$268,020
$2,500 Omaha Hi-Low Split	Eddie Fishman	$135,360
$1,500 Pot Limit Hold'em	John McIntosh	$177,380
$5,000 7-Card Stud	Qushqar Morad	$172,960
$2,000 S.H.O.E.	Phil Ivey	$107,540
$5,000 Limit Hold'em	Jennifer Harman	$221,440
$1,500 Limit Hold'em Shootout	Joel Chaseman	$96,400
$1,000 Ladies' Championship	Catherine Brown	$39,880
$5,000 Pot Limit Omaha	Robert Williamson III	$201,160
$1,500 Limit Hold'em	Meng La	$190,920

$5,000 Omaha Hi-Low Split	Mike Matasow	$148,520
$3,000 No Limit Hold'em	Randal Heeb	$367,240
$2,000 ½ Hold'em, ½ Stud	Dan Heimmer	$108,300
$5,000 No Limit 2-7 Draw	Allen Cunningham	$160,200
$1,000 Seniors' No Limit Championship	Bill Shan	$134,000
$1,500 Triple Draw Lowball	John Juanda	$490,620
Ace to Five		

Robert Varkonyi won a $1,100 one-table satellite to get into the WSOP main event.

1989 WSOP Champion Phil Hellmuth said of amateur Robert Varkonyi, "If he wins, I'll shave my head." Varkonyi won and Phil, being the good sport that he *always* is, posed for the cameras while Varkonyi, clippers in hand, sheepishly did the honors.

The hole card cam debuted on ESPN.

This was the first year that the WSOP used a $25,000 tournament chip.

This was the first year that the entire WSOP was a non-smoking event.

All nine players to make the final table autographed the poker table felt.

After the play got head up between Varkonyi and Gardner, it took 7 ½ hours and 161 hands to determine a winner.

WSOP Champion Robert Varkonyi named his daughter Victoria in honor of his victory.

Julian Gardner's nickname is "The Harry Potter of Poker."

Robert Varkonyi currently lives in Great Neck, New York, with his wife Olga.

2002 – Lyle Berman and Johnny Chan were inducted into the Poker Hall of Fame.

2003
34ᵀᴴ WORLD SERIES OF POKER
Christopher "Chris" Bryan Moneymaker

Winner: Chris Moneymaker
Runner-up: Sammy Farha
# of Players: 839
Prize: $2,500,000

The Final Hand:

Odds:		Pre-flop/	Flop/	Turn
Moneymaker	4♠ 5♦	35.49	91.82	81.82
Board:	4♣ 5♠ 8♦ J♠ 5♥			
Farha	J♥ T♦	63.31	6.57	18.18

The final table was:

1ˢᵗ	Chris Moneymaker	$2,500,000
2ⁿᵈ	Sammy Farha	$1,300,000
3ʳᵈ	Dan Harrington	$650,000
4ᵗʰ	Jason Lester	$440,000
5ᵗʰ	Tomer Benvenisti	$320,000
6ᵗʰ	Amir Vahedi	$250,000
7ᵗʰ	Young Pak	$200,000
8ᵗʰ	David Grey	$160,000
9ᵗʰ	David Singer	$120,000

The rest of the WSOP's events winners were:

$500 Casino Employees Limit Hold'em	David Lukaszewski	$35,800
$2,000 Limit Hold'em	Muhammad Ibrahim	$290,420
$1,500 7-Card Stud	Toto Leonidas	$98,760
$2,000 Omaha Hi-Low Split	Chris Ferguson	$123,680

$2,000 No Limit Hold'em	Jim Meehan	$280,100
$1,500 Pot Limit Hold'em	Prahiad Friedman	$109,400
$1,500 7-Card Stud Hi-Low Split	Minh Nguyen	$106,020
$1,500 Pot Limit Omaha	Erik Seidel	$146,000
$2,000 H.O.R.S.E.	Doyle Brunson	$84,080
$2,000 ½ Hold'em, ½ Stud	Chris Ferguson	$66,220
$2,500 No Limit Hold'em	Phi Nguyen	$222,800
$2,500 Limit Hold'em	Phil Hellmuth	$171,400
$2,500 7-Card Stud	Michael Saltzburg	$98,580
$5,000 No Limit 2-7 Draw	O'Neil Longson	$147,680
$5,000 No Limit Hold'em	Johnny Chan	$224,400
$1,500 Limit Omaha	Eddy Scharf	$63,600
$1,500 Limit Hold'em	John Arrage	$178,600
$5,000 7-Card Razz	Huck Seed	$71,500
$2,500 Omaha Hi-Low Split	Layne Flack	$119,260
$2,000 Pot Limit Hold'em	Mickey Appleman	$147,280
$1,000 Senior's No Limit Hold'em	Ron Rose	$130,060
$2,500 7-Card Stud Hi-Low Split	John Juanda	$130,200
$1,500 No Limit Hold'em	Amir Vahedi	$270,000
$2,000 S.H.O.E.	Daniel Negreanu	$100,440
$5,000 Pot Limit Omaha	Johnny Chan	$158,100
$1,500 Limit Hold'em Shootout	Layne Flack	$120,000
$3,000 Limit Hold'em	Tom Jacobs	$163,000
$1,000 Ladies' ½ Hold'em ½ Stud	Barb Rugolo	$40,700
$1,500 Omaha Hi-Low Split	Frankie O'Dell	$133,760
$3,000 Pot Limit Hold'em	Charles Keith Lehr	$225,040
$5,000 7-Card Stud	Men Nguyen	$178,560
$3,000 No Limit Hold'em	Phil Hellmuth	$410,860
$2,500 Pot Limit Omaha	John Juanada	$203,840
$5,000 Limit Hold'em	Juan Carlos Mortensen	$251,860
$1,500 Ace to Five Triple Draw Lowball	Men Nguyen	$43,520

Chris Moneymaker earned his $2,500,000 first prize money by winning a series of satellites, starting with a $39 buy-in on-line tournament.

A record fifty-one players got their $10,000 buy-in into the WSOP main event by winning internet tournaments.

After getting head-up with a 2-1 chip lead over Sammy Farha, Chris offered to split the first and second place money evenly. Sammy, being a pro and seeing that he was head-up against an amateur, turned down the offer.

Chris' name actually is Moneymaker. His ancestors made gold and silver coins and gave themselves the surname Nurmacher, which is German for Moneymaker.

1976-'77 WSOP Champion Doyle Brunson busted out of the 2003 WSOP main event while holding K♥9♥.

1989 WSOP Champion Phil Hellmuth busted out in 27th place while holding A♠K♦.

The last surviving WSOP Champion to be busted out was 1995 WSOP Champion Dan Harrington. He went out in 3rd place while holding K♦6♠.

Last year's champion Robert Varkonyi had a good chance to repeat this year until his pocket K♥K♦ was beat by Scotty Nguyen's A♦A♠ very late in the tournament.

During the tournament Chris Moneymaker knocked out Phil Ivey, Johnny Chan, David Grey, Tomer Benvenisti, Dan Harrington and Sammy Farha.

At one point early in the tournament, Johnny Chan held 5♠5♣ and flopped 2♣ 3♣ 4♣ for an open-end straight flush draw. He folded the hand rather than call a big bet that would have put him almost all-in.

The last female player to bust out of the main event was Annie Duke, who won $20,000 for going out in 47th place.

Chris Moneymaker is a celebrity spokesman for Harrah's Entertainment.

2003, December 5th – 1984 World Series of Poker Champion Jack Keller died in Tunica, Mississippi.

> *No style, type or form of money management will*
> *work if you play a game of skill without the skill.*
> Ken Warren, 2003

2003 – The only states to not have any form of legal gambling or private charity gambling are Hawaii and Utah.

2003 – 1978 World Series of Poker Champion Bobby Baldwin is inducted into the Poker Hall of Fame.

2004
35ᵀᴴ WORLD SERIES OF POKER
Greg "Fossilman" Raymer

Winner: Greg Raymer
Runner-up: David Williams
# of Players: 2,576
Prize: $5,000,000

The Final Hand:

Odds:		Pre-Flop/	Flop/	Turn
Raymer	8♠ 8♦	69.81	66.36	79.55
Board:	5♠ 4♦ 2♦ 2♥ 2♣			
Williams	A♥ 4♠	29.79	31.01	20.45

The final table was:

1st	Greg Raymer	$5,000,000
2nd	David Williams	$3,500,000
3rd	Josh Arieh	$2,500,000
4th	Dan Harrington	$1,500,000
5th	Glenn Hughes	$1,100,000
6th	Al Krux	$800,000
7th	Matt Dean	$675,000
8th	Mattias Andersson	$575,000
9th	Michael McClain	$470,000

The rest of the WSOP's events winners were:

$500 Casino Employees Limit Hold'em	Carl Nessel	$40,000
$2,000 No Limit Hold'em	James Vogel	$400,000
$1,500 7-Card Stud	Ted Forrest	$111,440
$1,500 Limit Hold'em	Aaron Katz	$234,940
$1,500 Omaha Hi-Low Split	Curtis Bibb	$160,000
$1,500 Pot Limit Hold'em	Minh Nguyen	$155,420
$1,000 No Limit Hold'em	Gerry Drehobl	$365,900
$2,000 Pot Limit Omaha	Chau Giang	$187,920
$1,500 No Limit Hold'em	Scott Fishman	$300,000
$2,000 7-Card Stud Hi-Low Split	Cyndy Violette	$135,900
$2,500 Limit Hold'em	Eli Balas	$174,440
$2,000 H.O.R.S.E.	Scott Fishman	$100,200
$5,000 No Limit Hold'em	Thomas Keller	$382,020
$1,500 7-Card Hi-Low Split	Hasan Habib	$93,060
$2,000 Limit Hold'em	Daniel Negreanu	$169,100
$5,000 No Limit 2-7 Draw	Barry Greenstein	$296,200
$1,500 Limit Hold'em Shootout	Kathy Liebert	$110,180
$1,500 No Limit Hold'em Shootout	Phi Nguyen	$180,000
$2,000 Omaha Hi-Low Split	Annie Duke	$137,860
$1,000 Ladies Limit Hold'em	Crystal Doan	$58,530
$2,000 Pot Limit Hold'em	Antonio Esfandiari	$58,530
$5,000 Omaha Hi-Low Split	Brett Jungblut	$187,720
$1,500 No Limit Hold'em	Ted Forrest	$300,300
$5,000 7-Card Stud	Joe Awada	$221,000
$3,000 Pot Limit Hold'em	Gavin Griffin	$270,420
$1,500 7-Card Razz	T.J. Cloutier	$900,500
$1,000 2-7 Triple Draw	Rarzad Bonyado	$86,980
$1,000 Senior's No Limit Hold'em	Gary Gibs	$136,960
$5,000 Limit Hold'em	John Hennigan	$325,360
$3,000 No Limit Hold'em	Mike Sica	$503,160
$5,000 Pot Limit Omaha	Ted Lawson	$500,000
$1,500 Ace to Five Lowball	Norm Ketchum	$84,000
Media Charity Event	Michael Kaplan	$10,000

WSOP organizers expected a total of 1,400 entrants in the main event this year but instead got a whopping 2,576 players.

912 players won their WSOP main event seat through an on-line tournament.

Stu Ungar's daughter Stephanie had the honor of starting this year's event by announcing, "Shuffle up and deal."

Greg Raymer won his entry into the WSOP by winning a $160 on-line satellite.

Greg Raymer says he's allergic to alcohol.

Greg Raymer currently resides in Raleigh, North Carolina.

2004 – Gus Hansen was named one of *People Magazine's* 50 Sexiest Men Alive.

2004 – IRS seizures ($1,000,000 to satisfy unpaid union benefits) forced the closure of Binion's Horseshoe. It was sold to Harrah's Entertainment and now operates as Binion's Gambling Hall and Hotel. It's owned by Terry Lynn Claudill, who also owns the 4 Queens Casino, which is just across the street from the property.

2004 – The World Series of Poker itself is owned and operated by Harrah's License Company, L. L. C., an affiliate of Harrah's Entertainment, Inc.

Hate the process—love the result.

> Tom McEvoy, 2004
> On writing poker books

2004, September 1st—The World Series of Poker Tournament of Champions held their first tournament. Annie Duke won the $2,000,000 first place (and only) prize.

2004, September 18th—The European Poker Tour held their first tournament.

2004, October – Paradise Poker was bought by SportingBet for $297,500,000.

2004 – WSOP Player of the Year was Daniel Negreanu.

2004 – 1986 World Series of Poker Champion Berry Johnston was inducted into the Poker Hall of Fame.

2005
36TH WORLD SERIES OF POKER
Joseph Hachem

2005, July 15th
Winner: Joe Hachem
Runner-up: Steve Dannenmann
# of Players: 5,619
Prize: $7,500,000

The Final Hand:

Odds:		Pre-flop/	Turn/	River
Hachem	7♣ 3♠	25.96	83.33	93.18
Board:	6♥ 5♦ 4♦ A♠ 4♣			
Dannenmann	A♦ 3♣	72.48	4.55	00.0

The final table was:

1st	Joseph "Joe" Hachem	$7,500,000
2nd	Steve Dannemann	$4,250,000
3rd	John "Tex" Barch	$2,500,000
4th	Aaron Kanter	$2,000,000
5th	Andrew Black	$1,750,000
6th	Scott Lazar	$1,500,000
7th	Daniel Bergsdorf	$1,300,000
8th	Brad Kondracki	$1,150,000
9th	Mike Matusow	$1,000,000

The rest of the WSOP's events winners were:

$500 Casino Employees No Limit Holdem	Andy Nguyen	$83,390
$1,500 No Limit Hold'em	Allen Cunningham	$725,405
$1,500 Pot Limit Hold'em	Thom Werthmann	$369,535
$1,500 Limit Hold'em	Eric Froehlich	$361,910

$1,500 Omaha Hi-Low Split	Pat Poels	$270,100
$2,500 Short Handed NL Hold'em	Isaac Galazan	$315,125
$1,000 No Limit Hold'em	Michael Gracz	$594,460
$1,500 7-Card Stud	Cliff Josephy	$192,150
$2,000 No Limit Hold'em	Erik Seidel	$611,195
$2,000 Limit Hold'em	Reza Payvar	$303,610
$2,000 Pot Limit Hold'em	Edward Moncada	$298,070
$2,000 Pot Limit Omaha	Josh Arieh	$381,600
$5,000 No Limit Hold'em	T.J. Cloutier	$657,100
$1,000 7-Card Stud Hi-Low	Steve Hohn	$156,986
$1,500 Limit Hold'em Shootout	Mark Seif	$181,330
$1,500 Limit Hold'em Shootout	Anthony Reategui	$269,100
$2,500 Limit Hold'em	Quinn Do	$265,975
$1,500 Pot Limit Omaha	Barry Greenstein	$128,505
$2,000 7-Card Stud Hi-Low	Denis Ethier	$160,682
$5,000 Pot Limit Hold'em	Brian Wilson	$370,685
$2,500 Omaha Hi-Low Split	Todd Brunson	$255,945
$1,500 No Limit Hold'em	Mark Seif	$611,145
$5,000 7-Card Stud	Jan Vang Sorensen	$293,275
$2,500 No Limit Hold'em	Farzad Bonyadi	$594,960
$2,500 Pot Limit Hold'em	Johnny Chan	$303,025
$5,000 Pot Limit Omaha	Phil Ivey	$635,603
$1,000 Ladies' No Limit Hold'em	Jennifer Tilly	$158,335
$5,000 Limit Hold'em	Dan Schmiech	$404,585
$2,000 No Limit Hold'em	Lawrence Gosney	$483,195
$1,500 7-Card Stud	O'Neil Longson	$125,960
$5,000 Short Handed NL Hold'em	Doyle Brunson	$367,800
$5,000 Omaha Hi-Low Split	David Chiu	$347,410
$3,000 No Limit Hold'em	Andre Boyer	$682,810
$1,000 Senior's No Limit Hold'em	Paul McKinney	$202,725
$10,000 Pot Limit Omaha	Rafi Amit	$511,835
$3,000 Limit Hold'em	Todd Witteles	$347,385
$1,000 No Limit Hold'em	Jiang Chen	$611,015
$1,000 Main Event Satellite		
$5,000 No Limit 2-7 Draw Lowball	David Grey	$365,135
$1,000 Main Event Satellite		
Media/Celebrity Charity Event	Randy Boman	$10,000
$10,000 World Championship	Joe Hachem	$7,500,000
No Limit Hold'em Main Event		

$1,500 No Limit Hold'em	Ron Kirk	$321,250
$1,000 No Limit Hold'em	John Pires	$220,935
$1,000 No Limit Hold'em	Willie Tann	$188,335

2005, June 27th—Jennifer Tilly became the first professional Hollywood actor/actress to win a WSOP bracelet.

Even though 5,619 players played in the main event, an additional 42 players registered but did not play.

Two on-line qualifiers died before the main event started.

Ten of the on-line qualifiers turned out to be underage and were denied a seat in the main event.

The website PokerStars sent a whopping 1,116 players to the main event.

This was the first year that all players who made the final table were paid $1,000,000 or more.

Harrah's bought the rights to the WSOP from the Binion family earlier this year.

Australian chiropractor Joe Hachem won the WSOP title and $7,500,000—almost matching the entire amount all players were paid when Chris Moneymaker won the title in 2003.

The first three days of the event were held at the RIO Casino and the final two days were moved back to Binion's Horseshoe.

Johnny Chan became the first player to win 10 WSOP bracelets.

The final event featured the longest head-up match in WSOP history when it took over six hours to play 232 hands.

Bear in mind that your own resolution to succeed
is more important than any other thing.

Abraham Lincoln, 1861

Every WSOP open event was won by a man this year.

Doyle and Todd Brunson became the first father-son to win WSOP bracelets. Doyle won the main event in 1976-77. Todd won the 2005 Omaha High-Low event.

1983 WSOP Champion Tom McEvoy busted out while holding A♠ Q♥.

Mike Matusow was given four ten-minute penalties for using the 'f-word.'

Greg Raymer was the last former champion to be busted out this year. He held K♦K♥ and was ahead after the flop. His opponent then hit running hearts (22-1 against) to make a flush, and he busted out in 25th place, winning $304,680. This was a stunningly impressive achievement because in two consecutive years, he finished 1st and 25th against a total of 8,193 opponents.

2005, February 15th – Two of Cassius Coolidge's "Dogs Playing Poker" paintings, *A Bold Bluff* and *Waterloo: Two*, went to auction expecting to sell for as much as $50,000. They instead sold for $590,400.

2005, March 4-6—The National Heads-Up Poker Championship held their first tournament. Phil Hellmuth defeated Chris Ferguson 2-1 for the championship.

2005 – The WSOP Player of the Year was Allen Cunningham.

Joe Hachem currently resides in Melbourne, Australia.

2005 – The Poker Channel and Pokerzone began broadcasting in Europe.

2005 – Jack Binion and Crandell Addington were inducted into the Poker Hall of Fame.

2005—A nationwide survey by a research company called Strategy One revealed that the one person that men would most like to play against was President George W. Bush. The women's top choice was Oprah Winfrey.

2006
37TH WORLD SERIES OF POKER
Jamie M. Gold

Date: August 10th, 2006
Winner: Jamie Gold
Runner-up: Paul Wasicka
#of Players: 8,773
Prize: $12,000,000

The Final Hand:

Odds:		Pre-flop/	Flop/	Turn
Gold	Q♠ 9♣	28.58	86.46	95.45
Board:	Q♣ 8♥ 5♥ A♦ 4♣			
Wasicka	T♠ T♥	71.02	13.54	4.55

The final table was:

1st	Jamie Gold	$12,000,000
2nd	Paul Wasicka	$6,102,499
3rd	Michael Binger	$4,123,310
4th	Allen Cunningham	$3,628,513
5th	Rhett Butler	$3,216,513
6th	Richard Lee	$2,803,851
7th	Douglas Kim	$2,391,520
8th	Erik Friberg	$1,979,189
9th	Dan Nassif	$1,566,858

The rest of the WSOP's events winners were:

$500 Casino Employees	Chris Gross	$127,616
No Limit Hold'em		
$1,500 No Limit Hold'em	Brandon Cantu	$755,839
$1,500 Pot Limit Hold'em	Rafe Furst	$345,984

$1,500 Limit Hold'em	Kianoush Abolfathi	$335,298
$2,500 No Limit Hold'em	Dutch Boyd	$475,712
Short Handed 6 Table		
$2,000 No Limit Hold'em	Mark Vos	$803,274
$3,000 Limit Hold'em	William Chen	$343,618
$2,000 Omaha Hi-Lo 8/B	Jack Zwerner	$341,426
$5,000 No Limit Hold'em	Jeff Cabamillas	$818,546
$1,500 7-Card Stud	David Williams	$163,118
$1,500 No Limit Hold'em	Bob Chalmers	$258,344
$5,000 Omaha Hi-Low 8/B	Sammy Farha	$398,560
$2,500 Limit Omaha	Max Pescatori	$628,389
$1,000 No Limit Hold'em	Allen Cunningham	$625,830
w/Multiple Rebuys		
$1,000 Ladies' No Limit Hold'em	Mary Jones	$236,094
$10,000 Pot Limit Omaha	Lee Watkinson	$655,746
$1,000 No Limit Hold'em	Jon Friedberg	$526,185
$2,000 Pot Limit Hold'em	Eric Keselman	$311,403
$1,000 Seniors' No Limit Hold'em	Clare Miller	$247,814
$50,000 H.O.R.S.E.	David "Chip" Reese	$1,716,000
$2,500 No Limit Hold'em	William Chen	$442,511
$2,000 No Limit Hold'em	Jeff Madsen	$660,948
$3,000 Limit Hold'em	Ian Johns	$291,755
$3,000 Omaha Hi-Low 8/B	Scott Clements	$301,175
$2,000 No Limit Hold'em Shootout	David Pham	$240,222
$1,500 Pot Limit Omaha	Ralph Perry	$207,817
$1,500 Pot Limit Omaha w/R	Eric Froehlich	$299,675
$1,500 No Limit Hold'em	Matts Rahmn	$655,141
$5,000 7-Card Stud	Benjamin Linn	$256,620
$2,500 Pot Limit Hold'em	John Gale	$374,849
$5,000 No Limit Hold'em	Jeff Madsen	$643,381
Short Handed 6 Table		
$2,000 No Limit Hold'em	Justin Scott	$842,262
$5,000 Pot Limit Hold'em	Jason Lester	$550,746
$1,500 Razz	James Richburg	$139,576
$1,000 No Limit Hold'em	Phil Hellmuth	$631,863
w/Multiple Rebuys		
$1,000 7-Card Stud Hi-Low 8/B	Pat Poels	$172,091
$1,500 Limit Hold'em Shootout	Victoriana Perches	$157,338
$1,500 No Limit Hold'em	James Gorham	$765,226

$5,000 No Limit 2-7 Draw	Daniel Alaei	$430,698
$10,000 World Championship No Limit Hold'em	Jamie Gold	$12,000,000
$1,000 No Limit Hold'em	Praz Bansi	$230,209
$1,500 No Limit Hold'em	Paul Kobel	$316,114
$1,500 No Limit Hold'em	Jim Mitchell	$153,173
$1,500 No Limit Hold'em	Kevin Nathan	$171,987
$1,500 No Limit Hold'em	Kevin Cover	$196,968
$1,500 No Limit Hold'em	Anders Henriksson	$202,291

This was the first year that the entire WSOP was held in a venue other than Binion's Horseshoe. All events were held at the Rio in Las Vegas.

Jamie Gold's birth name was Jamie Usher but his name was changed when his mother remarried.

WSOP Champion Jamie Gold's win of $12,000,000 set a record for the biggest monetary prize for any sport or event in the world.

Jamie Gold knocked out 7 of 8 of his final table opponents.

Jamie Gold was prevented by court order from collecting half of his WSOP winnings until he settled a dispute with an alleged partner. They settled with undisclosed terms in February, 2007.

This year saw the introduction of the "all-in" chip. Players were allowed to throw this single chip into the pot instead of pushing their entire stack in when going all-in.

Johnny Chan owns a fast food franchise in the Stratosphere Hotel and Casino.

Chip Reese wins the first $50,000 WSOP H.O.R.S.E event, along with $1,717,000 in first-place money. His A♣ Q♣ held up against Andy Bloch's 9♣ 8♠ when the board came J♠ 7♣ 7♠ 4♥ 4♠.

This year's H.O.R.S.E. event became the longest event in WSOP history when it took seven hours to play 286 hands.

In every battle there comes a time when both sides consider themselves beaten, then he who continues the attack wins.

Ulysses S. Grant, 1885

For the second consecutive year, every open event in this year's WSOP was won by a man.

With 8,733 entrants, this year's WSOP main event had the largest field ever.

A $100,000 tournament chip was used for the first time this year. It was mint green with black edge spots.

Gold's $12,000,000 was the largest prize for any competition worldwide, poker or otherwise.

The 2006 WSOP paid out a total of $156,409,974.

A record 666 players cashed in the main event this year.

This years' winner's bracelet was made by Frederick Goldman. It was made of 259 stones, including 7.2 carats of diamonds and 120 grains of white and yellow gold. The hearts and diamonds were made of rubies, the spade was made of sapphire and the clubs were made of three black diamonds.

Pro basketball player Charles Barkley, actor Tobey Maguire and boxer Lennox Lewis played in this year's WSOP main event.

1983 WSOP Champion Tom McEvoy busted out while holding 8♣ 8♦.

1989 WSOP Champion Phil Hellmuth and Humberto Brenes tied for the most number of cashes during on WSOP, with eight each.

2006, Jan 17th-Mar 14th—The William Hill Poker Grand Prix held their first tournament. Phil Laak was the winner.

2006, April 12th – 1973 World Series of Poker Champion Puggy Pearson died.

2006 – T.J. Cloutier and Billy Baxter were inducted into the Poker Hall of Fame.

2006 – The WSOP Player of the Year was Jeff Madsen.

2006 – Jeff Madsen became the youngest-yet player to win a WSOP bracelet. He was 21 years, one month and nine days old when he won the $2,000 No Limit Hold'em event. It paid $660,948.

2007
38TH WORLD SERIES OF POKER
Xao "Jerry the Shadow" Yang

Date: July 18th, 2007
Winner: Jerry Yang
Runner-up: Tuan Lam
# of Players: 6,358
Prize: $8,250,000

The Final Hand:

Odds:		Pre-flop/	Flop/	Turn
Yang	8♣ 8♦	52.56	16.36	13.64
Board	Q♣ 9♣ 5♠ 7♦ 6♥			
Lam	A♦ Q♦	47.01	83.64	86.36

The final table was:

1st	Jerry Yang	$8,250,000
2nd	Tuan Lam	$4,840,981
3rd	Raymond Rahme	$3,048,025
4th	Alex Kravchenko	$1,825,721
5th	Jon Kalmar	$1,255,069
6th	Hevad Khan	$956,243
7th	Lee Childs	$705,229
8th	Lee Watkinson	$585,699
9th	Philip Hilm	$525,934

The rest of the WSOP's events winners were:

$5,000 World Championship Mixed Hold'em	Steve Billirakis	$536,287
$500 Casino Employees No Limit Hold'em	Frederick Narciso	$104,701
$1,500 No Limit Hold'em	Ciaran O'Leary	$727,012
$1,500 Pot Limit Hold'em	Mike Spegal	$252,290
$2,500 Omaha/7-Card Stud Hi-Low 8/B	Tom Schneider	$214,347
$1,500 No Limit Hold'em	Gary Styczynski	$280,715
$5,000 Pot Limit Omaha w/R	Burt Boutin	$868,745
$1,000 No Limit Hold'em w/R	Michael Chu	$585,744
$1,500 Omaha Hi-Low 8/B	Alex Kravchenko	$228,446
$2,000 No Limit Hold'em	Will Durkee	$566,916
$5,000 World Championship 7-Card Stud	Chris Reslock	$258,435
$1,500 NL Hold'em Shorthanded	Jason Warner	$481,698
$5,000 World Championship Pot Limit Hold'em	Allen Cunningham	$487,287
$1,500 7-Card Stud	Michael Keiner	$146,987
$1,500 No Limit Hold'em	Phil Hellmuth	$637,254
$2,500 H.O.R.S.E.	James Richburg	$239,503
$1,000 World Championship Ladies' No Limit Hold'em	Sally Boyer	$262,077
$5,000 World Champion Limit Hold'em	Saro Getzoyan	$333,379
$2,500 No Limit Hold'em	Francois Safieddine	$521,785
$2,000 7-Card Stud H-L 8/B	Ryan Hughes	$176,358
$1,500 NL Hold'em Shootout	Don Baruch	$264,107
$5,000 No Limit Hold'em	James Mackey	$730,740
$1,500 Pot Limit Omaha	Scott Clements	$194,206
$3,000 World Championship 7-Card Stud Hi-Low 8/B	Eli Elezra	$198,984
$2,000 No Limit Hold'em	Ben Ponzio	$599,467
$5,000 H.O.R.S.E.	Ralph Schwartz	$275,683
$1,500 No Limit Hold'em	David Stucke	$603,069
$3,000 No Limit Hold'em	Shankar Pillai	$527,829
$1,500 7-Card Razz	Katja Thater	$132,635

$2,500 NL Hold'em Shorthanded	Hoyt Corkins	$515,065
$5,000 World Championship	Dan Schreiber	$425,594
$2,000 7-Card Stud	Jeffrey Lisandro	$118,426
$1,500 Pot Limit Omaha w/R	Alan Smurfit	$464,867
$3,000 Limit Hold'em	Alexander Borteh	$255,483
$1,500 No Limit Hold'em	Ryan Young	$615,955
$5,000 World Championship Omaha Hi-Low 8/B	John Guth	$363,216
$2,000 Pot Limit Hold'em	Greg Hopkins	$269,274
$1,500 No Limit Hold'em	Robert Cheung	$673,628
$50,000 World Championship H.O.R.S.E.	Freddy Deeb	$2,276,832
$1,500 Mixed Hold'em	Fred Goldberg	$204,935
$1,000 World Championship	Ernest Bennett	$348,423
$1,500 Pot Limit Omaha	Lukasz Dumanski	$277,454
$2,000 Limit Hold'em	Saif Ahmad	$217,329
$,2000 Omaha Hi-Low 8/B	Frankie O'Dell	$240,057
$5,000 NL Hold'em Shorthanded	Bill Edler	$904,672
$1,000 7-Card Stud HL 8/B	Tom Schneider	$147,713
$2,000 No Limit Hold'em	Blair Rodman	$707,898
$1,000 Limit 2-7 Triple Triple Draw Lowball w/R	Rafi Amit	$227,005
$1,500 No Limit Hold'em	Chandrasekhar Billavara	$722,914
$10,000 World Championship	Robert Mizrachi	$768,889
$1,000 S.H.O.E.	Dao Bac	$157,975
$1,000 No Limit Hold'em w/R	Michael Graves	$742,121
$1,000 NL Hold'em Shootout	Ram Vaswani	$217,438
$5,000 World Championship 2-7 Draw Lowball w/R	Erik Seidel	$538,835
$10,000 World Championship No Limit Hold'em Main Event	Jerry Yang	$8,250,000

Registration for the final event dropped from the previous year for only the second time in WSOP history. This year's entrants numbered just 6,358—down from 8,773 the previous year.

The ladies-only tournament set a record for number of players in a women's tournament at 1,286.

A total of 54,288 players played in all of this year's WSOP events. The total prize pool was $159,796,918.

This was the first year that all players started with a number of chips that was twice the buy-in.

Twenty former WSOP champions played in this year's WSOP main event. 1998 WSOP Scotty Nguyen lasted the longest, busting out on Day 6 in 11th place. He won $476,926.

Jason Holbrook, a blind player from California who had won his main event tournament seat through a satellite was denied permission to play by Harrah's.

2000 WSOP Champion Chris Ferguson busted out while holding A♦J♦.

Phil Hellmuth became the first player to win eleven WSOP bracelets. Unlike other multiple bracelet winners, *all eleven* of his are from Texas Hold'em events only.

Steve Billirakis, at age 21 years and 11 days, became the youngest person ever to win a WSOP bracelet.

CORUM became the official maker of WSOP bracelets.

The Ladies World Champion bracelet was made of four black diamonds, two rubies and 87 blue sapphires.

1989 WSOP Champion Phil Hellmuth arrived at this year's WSOP dressed as an 11-star army general—one star for each of his eleven bracelets.

The last woman eliminated was Maria Ho, who cashed in 38th place.

Annie Duke set the women's record with 33 WSOP cashes.

2006 WSOP Champion Jamie Gold busted out on the very first day of the event.

Just like last year's champion Jamie Gold, Jerry Yang knocked out 7 of 8 of his final table opponents.

2007 – The WSOP Player of the Year was Tom Schneider.

2007 – New Jersey banned smoking in 75% of the casino floors, while designating the other 25% to be either smoking rooms or floors.

I'm a pretty good poker player.

> Barack Obama, when asked by an AP
> reporter to name a hidden talent, 2007

2007 – Thomas Bihl became the first person to win a WSOP bracelet outside of Las Vegas. He won the inaugural WSOP Europe 2,500 pound buy-in event held in London.

2007, July 16th – Phil Hellmuth and Barbara Enright are inducted into the Poker Hall of Fame.

2007, September 17th – Annette Obrestad of Norway became the youngest player to win a WSOP bracelet, one day short of her 19th birthday. She won 1,000,000 pounds sterling ($2,010,000) in the inaugural WSOP Europe, where you only have to be 18 years old to play.

2007, November 10th—Harvard Law School held a conference to examine the possibility of using poker as a teaching tool.

Tom Schnieder was the WSOP player of the year. He won two events and made one other final table.

2008
39th WORLD SERIES OF POKER
Peter "Icegate" Eastgate

Winner:	Peter Eastgate
Runner-Up:	Ivan Demidov
# of Players:	6,844
Prize:	$9,152,416

The Final Hand:

Eastgate: A♦ 5♠

Board: 2♦ K♠ 3♥ 4♣ 7♠

Demidov: 4♥ 2♥

The final table was:

1st	Peter Eastgate	$9,152,416
2nd	Ivan Demidov	$5,790,024
3rd	Dennis Phillips	$4,503,352
4th	Ylon Schwartz	$3,763,515
5th	Scott Montgomery	$3,088,012
6th	Darius Suharto	$2,412,510
7th	David Rheem	$1,769,174
8th	Kelly Kim	$1,286,672
9th	Craig Marquis	$900,670

For the first time in WSOP history, play of the main event was suspended when the final nine players were determined. Play of the main event began on July 3rd and 6,844 players were reduced down to nine players on July 14th. Each of the nine players were then paid 9th place money. Play then resumed on November 9th and continued until that evening when the final two players were left. They then played heads-up on November 10th until a winner was determined.

The rest of the WSOP's events winners were:

$10,000 Championship Pot Limit Hold'em	Nenad Medic	$794,112
$1,500 No Limit Hold'em	Grant Hinkle	$831,462
$1,500 Pot Limit Hold'em	David Singer	$214,131
$5,000 Mixed Hold'em	Erick Lingren	$374,505
$1,000 No Limit Hold'em w/R	Michael Banducci	$636,736
$1,500 Omaha HL 8/B	Thang Luu	$243,356
$2,000 No Limit Hold'em	Matt Keikoan	$550,601
$10,000 World Championship Mixed Event	Anthony Rivera	$483,688
$1,500 No Limit Hold'em 6-Handed	Rep Porter	$327,929
$2,500 Omaha/7-Card Stud HL 8/B	Fredy Rouhani	$232,911
$5,000 NL Hold'em Shootout	Phil Tom	$477,990
$1,500 Limit Hold'em	Jimmy Shultz	$257,105
$2,500 No Limit Hold'em	Duncan Bell	$666,777
$10,000 World Championship 7-Card Stud	Eric Brooks	$415,586

$1,000 Ladies' NL Hold'em	Svetlana Gromenkova	$244,702
$2,000 Omaha HL 8/B	Andrew Brown	$286,483
$1,500 NL Hold'em Shootout	Jason Young	$335,565
$5,000 NL 2-7 Draw w/R	Mike Matusow	$537,826
$1,500 Pot Limit Omaha	Vanessa Selbst	$277,965
$2,000 Limit Hold'em	Daniel Negreanu	$204,874
$5,000 NL Hold'em	Scott Seiver	$755,891
$3,000 H.O.R.S.E.	Jens vortman	$298,253
$2,000 NL Hold'em	Blair Hinkle	$507,563
$2,500 Pot Limit Hold'em	Max Pescatori	$246,471
$10,000 World Championship Heads Up NL Hold'em	Kenny Tran	$539,056
$1,500 Razz	Barry Greenstein	$157,619
$1,500 NL Hold'em	Vitally Lunkin	$628,417
$5,000 Pot Limit Omaha w/R	Phil Galfond	$817,781
$3,000 NL Hold'em	John Phan	$434,789
$10,000 World Championship Heads Up Limit Hold'em	Rob Hollink	$496,931
$2,500 NL Hold'em 6-Handed	Dario Minieri	$528,418
$1,500 NL Hold'em	Luis Velador	4574,734
$5,000 7-Card Stud HL 8/B	Sebastian Ruthenberg	$328,756
$1,500 Pot Limit Omaha w/R	Layne Flack	$577,725
$1,500 7-Card Stud	Michael Rocco	$135,735
$1,500 NL Hold'em	David Woo	$631,656
$10,000 World Championship Omaha HL 8/B	David Benyamine	$535,687
$2,000 Pot Limit Hold'em	Davidi Kitai	$244,583
$1,500 NL Hold'em	David Woo	$631,656
$2,500 2-7 Limit Triple Draw	John Phan	$151,896
$1,500 Mixed Hold'em	Frank Gary	$219,508
$1,000 Senior's NL Hold'em World Championship	Dan Lacourse	$368,832
$1,500 Pot Limit Omaha HL 8/B	Martin Klaser	$216,249
$1,000 No Limit Hold'em w/R	Max Greenwood	$693,444
$50,000 World Championship H.O.R.S.E.	Scotty Nguyen	$1,989,120
$5,000 No Limit Hold'em 6-Handed	Joe Commisso	4911,855
$1,500 7-Card Stud HL 8/B	Ryan Hughes	$183,368
$2,000 No Limit Hold'em	Alexandre Gomes	$770,540

$1,500 No Limit Hold'em	J.C. Tran	$631,170
$10,000 World Championship Pot Limit Omaha	Marty Smyth	$859,549
$1,500 H.O.R.S.E.	James Schaaf	$256,412
$1,500 No Limit Hold'em	David Daneshgar	$625,443
$1,500 Limit Hold'em Shootout	Mark Graham	$278,180
$10,000 World Championship No Limit Hold'em Main Event	Peter Eastgate	$9,119,517
$500 Casino Employees	Jonathan Kotula	$87,929

At age 22 years, 10 months and 28 days, Peter Eastgate is the youngest-ever winner of the WSOP main event.

The average age of the players at the main event final table was 35 years old, compared to 45 in 1970.

Dewey Tomko holds the record for the longest active streak of playing 35 consecutive years in the main event. He finished second to Jack Straus in 1982 and second again to Carlos Mortensen in 2001. He busted out on the bubble two other times.

This year's WSOP broke three big records:

Most entries: 58,720
Most countries: 124 represented
Prize pool: $180,774,427

This ain't the internet.

Mike Matusow, 2008
On the size of the WSOP field

This year's WSOP was opened by "Mr. Las Vegas" Wayne Newton.

A record 209 women entered the final event.

Jack Ury, from Terre Haute, Indiana is the oldest player to play in the WSOP main event, at age 95.

Players in the WSOP main event are allowed to wear headphones, listen to i-pods and the like only until the last non-paid player busts out. Once all players are in the money, all headphones must come off.

Phil Hellmuth has made a record 41 final tables in WSOP events.

The last WSOP bracelet winner to bust out was Brandon Cantu. He went out in 20th place, earning $257,344.

Nikolay Evdakov set a WSOP record when he cashed in ten bracelet events, all without reaching a single final table.

2008—Of the 24 living past World Series of Poker Main Event Champions, 20 of them played in this year's main event. The four to not play were Russ Hamilton, Humberto Brenes, Mansour Matloubi and Amarillo Slim Preston.

1983 WSOP Champion Tom McEvoy busted out while holding J♦T♦.

1987-'88 WSOP Champion Johnny Chan busted out while holding A♠7♥. He lost to 8♦8♥.

1989 WSOP Champion Phil Hellmuth busted out in 45th place out of 6,844 players while holding A♥Q♦. His opponent held J♥J♣ while the board was 4♥ K♦ 3♥ T♥ 2♠. He cashed for $154,400.

1996 WSOP Champion Huck Seed busted out while holding A♥7♦.

1998 WSOP Champion Scotty Nguyen busted out while holding 9♣9♦. The board was A♥ 9♥ 4♥ 5♦ 7♥ and his opponent help K♣K♥.

2002 WSOP Champion Robert Varkonyi busted out on Day 2, hole cards unknown.

2003 WSOP Champion Chris Moneymaker busted out while holding A♥J♣. He was beat by T♠9♠. He has not cashed at the WSOP since his breakthrough win in 2003.

2005 WSOP Champion Joe Hachem busted out while holding J♣6♣. The board was 5♣ 2♣ 2♠ Q♥ J♥ and his opponent held Q♠ Q♣.

2006 WSOP Champion Jamie Gold busted out on Day 1.

2007 WSOP Jerry Yang busted out while holding AJ♣. The board was 5♣ 9♥ 4♠ Q♣ and his opponent held A♦J♣.

Actor Ray Romano busted out on Day 2 while holding 8♠8♣. The board was 7♥ 4♣ 2♥ 9♥ 4♠ and his opponent held A♥3♥.

Phil Ivey busted out while holding K♣Q♠.

Mike Matusow busted out while holding A♦J♣. The board was A♥ A♠ 5♦ K♠ 9♥ and his opponent held A♣9♣.

All players started with $20,000 in tournament chips instead of the traditional $10,000.

Seinfeld star Jason Alexander busted out while holding A♦A♥, thereby losing a $1,000 'last longer' bet to *Everybody Loves Raymond* star Ray Romano.

2008—First time in WSOP history a player made four Aces while holding pocket Aces and lost to a royal flush. The odds against that are 7,700,000 to 1.

Daniel Negreanu busted out while holding 6♣6♠. He made a set of 6s but lost to a set of 9s.

2008 – The WSOP Player of the Year was Eric Lindgren.

Eric Lindgren was best man at Daniel Negreanu's wedding. Daniel is now divorced.

The RIO's Amazon Room can accommodate 2,740 poker players.

The last three female players to bust out were:

Tiffany Michelle, 17th place, $334,534,
Lisa Parsons, 76th place, $77,200,
Kara Scott, 104th place, $41,816

Tiffany Michelle is a certified massage therapist.

Phil Hellmuth holds the record for the most final table appearances at WSOP events at 41, and he also holds the record for the most WSOP cashes at 68.

For the first time ever, two brothers won bracelets at the WSOP:

Grant Hinkle, Event #2, $2,000 buy-in No-Limit Hold'em, $500,000
Blair Hinkle, Event #23, $1,500 buy-in No-Limit Hold'em, $800,000

The WSOP introduced a beige $250,000 tournament chip.

For the first time, the big blind in the main event reached $1,000,000 in tournament chips.

After nine players made the final table, it took 274 hands and 15 hours and 28 minutes to determine a winner. The final head-up action lasted a little more than four hours and took 105 hands.

Johnny Chan has played in every WSOP main event since 1992 but did not cash until this year. He took 329th place for a win of $32,166.

The 2008 WSOP main event 'bubble boy' was Steve Chung. The event paid 666 places and he busted out in 667th place while holding 8♥8♣. His opponent held K♠K♦ and the board was 2♥ J♥ 2♣ 3♥ 6♠. He missed being paid $21,230 by one place.

2008 – Dewey Tomko and Henry Orenstein were inducted into the Poker Hall of Fame.

2008 – Phil Hellmuth has won 11 WSOP bracelets and has given away 10 of them. He said, "To me, the bracelets have always been a really huge deal, to me more than the other guy, because I know that they represent history."

Most cashes in WSOP history, going into the 2009 WSOP:

67	Phil Hellmuth, Jr.
61	Men Nguyen
57	Berry Johnston
55	Chris Ferguson
54	T.J. Cloutier
53	Humberto Brenes

2008 – The David "Chip" Reese Award Trophy is created for the winner of the annual $50,000 buy-in H.O.R.S.E. event. The first winner of the award was Scotty Nguyen.

2008 – Scotty Nguyen is the only player to win a WSOP main event (1998) and the $50,000 buy-in H.O.R.S.E. title (2008).

2008, February 2nd – Barbara Enright was inducted into the Women In Poker Hall of Fame. She is the only person enshrined in the WSOP Hall of Fame, The Senior Poker Hall of Fame and the Women In Poker Hall of Fame.

2008 – John Juanda is the first American WSOP Europe main event champion. He won the final hand with four 6s.

2008, May—The Latin American Poker Tour held their first tournament in Rio de Janeiro, Brazil.

2008, December 28th – Poker Stars hosted the largest on-line poker tournament ever. It had 35,000 players, an $11 buy-in, took 9 ½ hours to play, paid 8,750 places and paid $30,000 to first-place finisher "Stan34powa" from France.

2008 – A standard deck of playing cards can be shuffled into 80,658,175,170,943,878,571,660,636,856,404,000,000,000,000,000 different permutations.

2008, December 31st – The #1 most popular internet search term for 2008 was POKER.

2008, December 31st—The 91 poker rooms in California took in $800,000,000, more than five times the $156,000,000 that the 106 Nevada poker rooms took in.

2009
40th WORLD SERIES OF POKER
Joseph Cada

November 10, 2009
Winner: Joseph Cada
Runner-up: Darvin Moon
# of Players: 6,494
1st Place $: $8,546,435

Cada: 9♣9♦

Board: 8♣ 7♠ 2♣ K♥ 7♣

Moon: Q♦J♦

The final table was:

1st	Joe Cada	$8,546,435
2nd	Darvin Moon	$5,182,601
3rd	Antoine Saout	$3,479,485
4th	Eric Buchman	$2,502,787
5th	Jeff Shulman	$1,953,395
6th	Steve Bergleiter	$1,587,133
7th	Phil Ivey	$1,404,002
8th	Kevin Schaffel	$1,300,228
9th	James Ankenhead	$1,263,602

Preliminary event winners for the 2009 WSOP:

Event	Winner	1st Place Prize Money
$500 Casino Employees No Limit Hold'em	Andrew Cohen	$83,788
$40,000 NL Hold'em	Vitaly Lunkin	$1,891,021
$1,500 Omaha H/L 8/B	Thang Luu	$263,135
$1,000 No Limit Hold'em	Steve Sung	$771,106
$1,500 Pot Limit Hold'em	Jason Mercier	$237,415

$10,000 World Champion ship 7-Card Stud	Freddie Ellis	$373,744
$1,500 No Limit Hold'em	Travis Johnson	$666,853
$2,500 2-7 Lowball	Phil Ivey	$96,361
$1,500 No Limit Hold'em Short Handed	Ken Aldridge	$428,259
$2,500 Pot Limit Hold'em/Omaha	Rami Boukai	$244,862
$2,000 No Limit Hold'em	Anthony Harb	$269,199
$10,000 World Championship Mixed Event*	Ville Wahlbeck	$492,275
$2,500 No Limit Hold'em	Kevin Stammen	$506,786
$2,500 Limit Hold'em Short Handed	Brock Parker	$223,688
$5,000 No Limit Hold'em	Brian Lemke	$629,659
$1,500 7-Card Stud	Jeff Lisandro	$124,959
$1,000 Ladies' No Limit Hold'em	Lisa Hamilton	$195,390
$10,000 World Champion ship Omaha H/L 8/B	Daniel Alaei	$445,898
$2,500 No Limit Hold'em Short Handed	Brock Parker	$522,745
$1,500 Pot Limit Hold'em	J.P. Kelly	$194,434
$3,000 H.O.R.S.E.	Zac Fellows	$311,899
$1,500 No Limit Hold'em Shootout	Jeff Carris	$313,673
$10,000 World Champion ship 2-7 Draw	Nick Schulman	$279,724
$1,500 No Limit Hold'em	Peter Vilandos	$607,256
$2,500 Omaha/7-Card Stud 8/B	Phil Ivey	$220,538
$1,500 Limit Hold'em	Tomas Alenius	$197,488
$5,000 Pot Limit Omaha H/L 8/B	Roland De Wolfe	$246,616
$1,500 No Limit Hold'em	Mike Eise	$639,331
$10,000 World Champion ship Heads-Up No Limit Hold'em	Leo Wolpert	$625,682
$2,500 Pot Limit Omaha	J.C. Tran	$235,685
$1,500 H.O.R.S.E	James Van Alstyne	$247,033
$2,000 No Limit Hold'em	Angel Guillen	$530,548
$10,000 Limit Hold'em World Championship	Greg Mueller	$460,836
$1,500 No Limit Hold'em	Eric Baldwin	$521,932
$5,000 Pot Limit Omaha	Richard Austin	$409,484
$2,000 No Limit Hold'em	Jordan Smith	$586,212

$10,000 7-Card Stud 8/B World Championship	Jeff Lisandro	$431,656
$2,000 Limit Hold'em	Marc Naalden	$190,770
$1,500 No Limit Hold'em	Ray Foley	$657,969
$10,000 Pot Limit Omaha World Championship	Matt Graham	$697,279
$5,000 No Limit Hold'em Shootout	Peter Traply	$348,728
$2,500 Mixed Event	Jerrod Ankenman	$241,654
$2,500 Razz	Jeff Lisandro	$188,370
$10,000 PL Hold'em World Championship	John Kabbaj	$633,335
$25,00 Omaha H/L 8/B	Derek Raymond	$229,192
$2,500 Mixed Hold'em	Bahador Ahmadi	$278,804
$1,500 Pot Limit Omaha H/L 8/B	Brandon Cantu	$228,876
$50,000 H.O.R.S.E. World Championship	David Bach	$1,276,802
$1,500 Limit Hold'em Shootout	Greg Mueller	$194,854
$1,500 No Limit Hold'em	Joh Carsten	$664,426
$3,000 Triple Chance No Limit Hold'em	Jorg Peisert	$506,800
$1,500 7-Card Stud H/L 8/B	David Halpern	$159,390
$1,500 No Limit Hold'em	Tony Veckey	$673,276
$2,500 207 Triple Draw Lowball	Abe Mosseri	$165,521
$5,000 No Limit Hold'em Short Handed	Matt Hawrilenko	$1,003,163
$1,000 Senior's No Limit Hold'em World Championship	Michael Davis	$437,358

*The $10,000 World Championship Mixed event consisted of the following games, with blinds, levels and games changing at one hour intervals: Limit 2-7 Triple Draw, Limit Hold'em, Limit Omaha H/L 8/B, Razz, 7-Card Stud, 7-Card Stud 8/B, NL Hold'em and Pot Limit Omaha.

The final event was played from Friday, July 3rd through July 15th, 2009. A total of 6,494 players entered the event, 648 places were paid and the final nine players continued play on Tuesday, November 10th, 2009. All nine players were paid 9th place money, since they were all guaranteed at least 9th place. Each player will be paid the additional difference between 9th place and their actual place, plus interest, as they bust out in November.

The nine remaining players and their chip counts going into the final table were:

1st	Darvin Moon	$58,930,000
2nd	Eric Buchman	$34,800,000
3rd	Steven Begleiter	$29,885,000
4th	Jeff Shulman	$19,580,000
5th	Joseph Cada	$13,215,000
6th	Kevin Schaffel	$12,390,000
7th	Phil Ivey	$9,765,000
8th	Antonio Saout	$9,500,000
9th	James Ankenhead	$6,800,000

This is how each player busted out at the final table:

Place	Loser	Loser's hand	The Board	Winner	Winner's hand
9th	Ankenhead	3♦3♣	T♣2♣7♥2♠9♦	Schaffel	9♠9♥
8th	Schaffel	A♥A♣	Q♣Q♥K♠K♦9♣	Buchman	K♥K♣
7th	Ivey	A♣K♠	6♣6♠Q♦3♣5♣	Moon	A♦Q♠
6th	Begleiter	Q♠Q♦	7♣4♦8♣3♦A♦	Moon	A♣Q♥
5th	Shulman	7♥7♣	T♣9♦6♣Q♣4♣	Saout	A♣9♠
4th	Buchman	A♦5♣	2♣9♥Q♣K♥5♥	Moon	K♦J♦
3rd	Saout	Q♦Q♥	7♣2♦9♣3♥6♣	Cada	2♣2♠

At one point, eventual winner Joe Cada was in 8th place with less than 1% of the chips in play, thus adding to the axiom, "All I need is a chip and a chair."

The average age of the players who made the final table was 34.5 years, compared to 45 years in 1970.

At the age of 21 years, 11 months and 21 days, Joe Cada became the youngest-ever winner of the WSOP main event. He is 340 days younger than previous record holder Peter Eastgate.

Life is only a game of poker, played well or ill;
Some hold four aces, some draw or fill;
Some make a bluff and oft get there,
While others ante and never hold a pair.

Pat Hogan
On the back of an A♥ found
Among his effects, 1892

2009, January 14th – Pennsylvania Columbia County Judge Thomas A. James, Jr., ruled that Texas Hold'em is a game of skill.

2009 – Huck Seed won the National Heads-Up Poker Championship and $500,000 by defeating Vanessa Rousso. The event was a 64-player, single-elimination, bracket-style format, except that the final match went to the best out of three.

2009 – This is the first year that the entire WSOP was an all no-rebuy event.

2009 – This, the 40th WSOP, had 57 bracelet events, the most ever.

2009 – Going into the 2009 WSOP, T.J. Cloutier has won more poker tournaments of all kinds in a lifetime than any other poker player in history.

2009, April 29th—The International Federation of Poker was created. It was founded in Lausanne, Switzerland and elected poker player/author Anthony Holden as its first president.

2009, June 2nd—1983 WSOP Champion Tom McEvoy won the inaugural WSOP Champions Invitational Tournament. Only former WSOP main event champions were eligible to play and the winner was awarded the Binion Cup and a red 1970 Corvette with no miles on the odometer, valued at $50,000. McEvoy defeated 19 former champions to win the event.

2009—The chip colors used in this year's WSOP main event were:

$25	Green
$100	Black
$500	Blue
$1,000	Yellow
$5,000	Orange
$25,000	Green
$100,000	Purple
$250,000	Beige

Note: The $25 green chips were raced off the table long before the $25,000 green chips are introduced, so there could not possibly be any confusion.

2009—For their $10,000 buy-in, all players at the main event each started with $30,000 in tournament chips, as opposed to $20,000 in 2008 and $10,000 in chips in 2007 and all previous years.

2009—Jack Urey, of Terre Haute, Indiana, played in the main event again this year at age 96.

2009—The 2009 WSOP main event bubble boy was Kia Hamadani, busting out in 649th place.

2009—Jeffrey Lisandro became only the fifth player to win three bracelets during one WSOP. This ties him with Puggy Pearson (1973), Ted Forrest (1993), Phil Hellmuth (1993) and Phil Ivey (2002).

2009—The last of last year's 'November 9' to bust out this year was Dennis Phillips. He held A♦K♦ while his opponent held A♠K♠. The board was 4♠ K♣ 6♠ T♥ 5♠. He busted out in 45th place and was paid $178,857.

1976-77 WSOP Champion Doyle Brunson busted out on Day 1 while holding 3♠3♥. The board was 9♥3♦7♠4♥A♦ and his opponent held 6♣5♣.

1987-88 WSOP Champion Johnny Chan busted out on Day 2 while holding A♥4♦. The board was 8♥K♥Q♠T♣Q♣ and his opponent held 9♥9♦.

1989 WSOP Champion Phil Hellmuth busted out in 436th place for a win of $25,027 while holding A♣A♠. Instead of going all-in before the flop or otherwise trying to narrow the field, he saw the flop 5-handed! The board was J♣T♦5♣7♦3♠ and one of his four opponents beat him while holding 9♥8♥. He then said, "These are some of the worst players in the entire world over here."

1995 WSOP Champion Dan Harrington busted out in 252nd place for a win of $32,963. It was his first cash in the main event since 2004.

1998 WSOP Champion Scotty Nguyen busted out on Day 2 while holding A♠A♥. The board was 5♥5♣T♣K♠K♣ and his opponent held K♥T♠.

2000 WSOP Champion Chris Ferguson busted out in 561st place, for a win of $23,196. He held 9♦2♥, the board was J♣6♦6♣8♦A♥ and his opponent held A♣6♥.

2003 WSOP Champion Chris Moneymaker busted out on Day 1 while holding T♠T♥. The board was 7♦Q♠9♣4♥Q♥ and his opponent held A♠A♣.

2005 WSOP Champion Joe Hachem busted out in 103rd place, for a win of $40,288 while holding J♣9♣. The board was K♣7♣7♠A♥3♥ and his opponent held 4♠4♣.

2007 WSOP Champion Jerry Yang busted out on Day 1 while holding J♦7♦. The board was 7♥9♥8♣K♦4♣ and his opponent held A♥K♠.

2008 WSOP Champion Peter Eastgate busted out in 78th place for a win of $68,979 while holding A♦J♠. The board was 6♦A♥4♥J♥3♥ while his opponent held 8♠8♥.

2009, July-November—Jeff Shulman hired 1989 WSOP Champion Phil Hellmuth to coach him for the final table.

Being world champion is still something special,
But it no longer means you are the best in the world.

Barny Boatman, 2009

2009—Players with the most WSOP bracelets without a main event title:

8	Erik Seidel
7	Phil Ivey
7	Billy Baxter
6	Men Nguyen
6	T.J. Cloutier
6	Layne Flack

2009—All-time top female main event finishers, as of 2009:

5th	Barbara Enright	1995
10th	Barbara Samuelson	1994
10th	Susie Issacs	1998
10th	Annie Duke	2000
12th	Marsha Waggoner	1997

The last two women to bust out of the 2009 main event were:

> Leo Margets, 27th place, $352,832
> Nichoel Peppe, 75th place, $68,979

2009, July 19th—The largest ever online Hold'em tournament took place on PokerStars.com. 65,000 players from 155 different countries paid $1 each to compete for a $13,000 first prize, which was eventually won by "004license" from South Carolina.

2009, August 1st—The television reality show *Face The Ace* debuted on NBC with *Sopranos* star Steve Schirripa as host and Ali Jejad as emcee.

2009 – The game of Texas Hold'em is illegal in the state of Texas except for two small poker rooms in the El Paso area.

2009, September—Harrah's Entertainment and ESPN signed a deal to ensure that coverage of the WSOP continues to be aired through the year 2018.

2009, September 6th—Internet poker site PokerStars set a world record, verified by Guinness Book of World Records, for the largest number of players playing poker at any one time at an internet poker room. A total of 307,016 players were playing at 42,814 tables at the same time.

2009, September 24th—Englishman Paul Zimbler set the world record for longest continuous poker session at 74 hours, 20 minutes and 21 seconds. He raised $60,000 for the Make-A-Wish Foundation. He won 102 of 183 matches.

2009 – Poker is the 3rd most watched televised event, trailing only auto racing and pro football.

2009 – The top five all-time WSOP bracelet winners are:

11	Phil Hellmuth
10	Johnny Chan
10	Doyle Brunson
9	Johnny Moss
8	Erik Seidel

Of the five players listed above, only Johnny Chan still has all of his bracelets.

Appendix I

WORLD SERIES OF POKER
ALL-TIME MONEY WINNERS

1st	Jamie Gold	$12,185,313
2nd	Daniel Negreanu	$11,251,996
3rd	Joseph Hachem	$10,601,419
4th	Scotty Nguyen	$10,217,869
5th	Allen Cunningham	$9,855,668
6th	Peter Eastgate	$9,657,466
7th	Phil Ivey	$9,606,333
8th	Erik Seidel	$9,208,245
9th	T.J Cloutier	$9,113,236
10th	John Juanda	$9,079,752

Appendix II

LIFETIME WSOP EARNINGS
OF EACH WSOP CHAMPION

These numbers are for WSOP events only. Almost all of these champions have played in other tournaments where they have won money. Those results are not included here.

1970	–	Johnny Moss	$824,922
1972	–	Amarillo Slim Preston	$436,748
1973	–	Puggy Pearson	$212,100
1975	–	Sailor Roberts	$267,650
1976	–	Doyle Brunson	$2,830,302
1978	–	Bobby Baldwin	$604,900
1979	–	Hal Fowler	$270,000
1980	–	Stu Ungar	$2,078,838
1982	–	Jack Straus	$555,000
1983	–	Tom McEvoy	$1,284,611
1984	–	Jack Keller	$1,583,845
1985	–	Bill Smith	$788,000
1986	–	Berry Johnston	$2,057,168

1987	–	Johnny Chan	$4,148,868
1989	–	Phil Hellmuth	$6,082,391
1990	–	Mansour Matloubi	$1,214,162
1991	–	Brad Daugherty	$1,158,574
1992	–	Hamid Dastmalchi	$1,600,760
1993	–	Jim Bechtel	$1,809,967
1994	–	Russ Hamilton	$1,261,940
1995	–	Dan Harrington	$3,491,940
1996	–	Huck Seed	$2,426,842
1998	–	Scotty Nguyen	$9,440,880
1999	–	Noel Furlong	$1,070,785
2000	–	Chris Ferguson	$4,008,303
2001	–	Carlos Mortensen	$2,153,935
2002	–	Robert Varkonyi	$2,051,398
2003	–	Chris Moneymaker	$2,532,041
2004	–	Greg Raymer	$5,712,585
2005	–	Joe Hachem	$7,941,823
2006	–	Jamie Gold	$12,067,929
2007	–	Jerry Yang	$8,250,000
2008	–	Peter Eastgate	$9,152,416
2009	--	Joe Cada	$8,546,435

Appendix III

WHAT THE WORLD SERIES OF POKER CHAMPIONSHIP WINNER'S LIST WOULD LOOK LIKE IF THE RUNNER-UP HAD WON

1970	None
1971	None
1972	Walter "Clyde" Puggy Pearson
1973	Johnny Moss
1974	None
1975	Bob Hooks
1976	Jesse Alto
1977	"Bones" Berland
1978	Crandell Addington
1979	Bobby Hoff

1980	Doyle Brunson
1981	Perry Green
1982	Dewey Tomko
1983	Rod Peate
1984	Byron "Cowboy" Wolford
1985	T. J Cloutier
1986	Mike Harthcock
1987	Frank Henderson
1988	Erik Seidel
1989	Johnny Chan
1990	Hans "Tuna" Lund
1991	Don Holt
1992	Tom Jacobs
1993	Glen Cozen
1994	Hugh Vincent
1995	Howard Goldfarb
1996	Dr. Bruce Van Horn
1997	John Strzemp
1998	Kevin McBride
1999	Alan Goehring
2000	T. J. Cloutier
2001	Dewey Tomko
2002	Julian Gardner
2003	Sammy Farha
2004	David Williams
2005	Steve Dannenmann
2006	Paul Wasicka
2007	Tuan Lam
2008	Ivan Demidov
2009	Darvin Moon

Appendix IV

OF WSOP PRELIMINARY EVENTS BY YEAR

1970 – 4	1980 – 11	1990 – 14	2000 – 24
1971 – 4	1981 – 11	1991 – 16	2001 – 25
1972 – unknown	1982—13	1992—19	2002—34
1973 – 7	1983 – 13	1993 – 18	2003 – 35
1974 – 5	1984 – 13	1994 – 20	2004 – 33
1975 – 4	1985 – 11	1995 – 23	2005 – 45
1976 – 7	1986 – 12	1996 – 23	2006 – 45
1977 – 12	1987 – 11	1997 – 20	2007 – 55
1978 – 10	1988 – 11	1998 – 20	2008 – 55
1979 – 11	1989 – 13	1999 – 15	2009 – 57

Appendix V

INTERESTING WSOP TRIVIA

Number of times each card has appeared on the board in all of the final hands:

A♣ 1	A♦ 4	A♥ 3	A♠ 2
K♣ 3	K♦ 3	K♥ 2	K♠ none
Q♣ 6	Q♦ 2	Q♥ 1	Q♠ 7
J♣ 2	J♦ 2	J♥ 1	J♠ 5
T♣ 5	T♦ 7	T♥ 3	T♠ 3
9♣ 5	9♦ 2	9♥ 5	9♠ 1
8♣ 6	8♦ 5	8♥ 5	8♠ 8
7♣ 2	7♦ 4	7♥ none	7♠ 1
6♣ none	6♦ 6	6♥ 4	6♠ 2
5♣ 3	5♦ 5	5♥ 5	5♠ 6
4♣ 4	4♦ 2	4♥ 4	4♠ 5
3♣ 6	3♦ 2	3♥ 1	3♠ 3
2♣ 8	2♦ 2	2♥ 4	2♠ 4

The K♠, 7♥ and 6♣ have never appeared on the board in a WSOP final hand while the 8♠ and 2♣ hold the record with eight appearances. There have been a total of 30 deuces and treys while there have been only 17 Aces and Kings. The reason for the big difference should be obvious: Players will more often go all-in and make a final stand while holding these two big cards. Cards that are in the players' hands obviously can't come on the board.

Number of winners who started the final hand with the best cards:

19 of 35 (54.73%)

Worst hole cards to win the WSOP:

5♠ 4♠ Stu Ungar in 1980
5♦ 4♠ Chris Moneymaker in 2003

Biggest underdogs to win the WSOP on the final hand before the flop:

2001—   Carlos Mortensen's K♣ Q♣ (17.5%) against
            Dewey Tomko's A♠ A♥ (82.13%)

1999—   Noel Furlong's 5♣ 5♦ (17.67%) against
            Alan Goehring's 6♥ 6♣ (80.39)

1979—   Hal Fowler's 7♠ 6♦ (19.22%) against
            Bobby Hoff's A♥ A♣ (80.52)

Number of winners who held a pocket pair in the final hand of the WSOP:

11 of 35 (29.41%)

Number of winners who held an Ace and another card in the final hand of the WSOP:

7 of 34 (20.58%)

Winners who held the worst hand going into the river:

Jack Straus was losing after the turn and had exactly three outs (T♠, T♦, T♥) to win it on the river. He got the T♠.

Chris Ferguson was losing after the turn and had exactly three outs (9♥, 9♠, 9♦) to win it on the river. He got the 9♥.

Winners who had the nuts on the turn and could not be beat no matter what card came on the river:

Hal Fowler—1979
Johnny Chan—1988
Joe Hachem—2005

Highest poker hand to win the WSOP:

A full house consisting of Tens full of Deuces by Doyle Brunson in 1976....and 1977!

Lowest poker hand to win the WSOP:

J♣ T♦ 8♠ 6♥ 5♦ made by Jim Bechtel in 1993 while holding J♣ 6♥. Glen Cozen held 7♠ 4♦ and couldn't beat it.

Highest poker hand to lose on the final hand of the WSOP:

David Williams made a 4♠ 4♦ 2♦ 2♣ 2♥ full house only to lose to Greg Raymer's higher full house of 8♠ 8♦ 2♦ 2♣ 2♥ in 2004.

Kevin McBride played the full house on the board—8♣ 9♦ 9♥ 8♥ 8♠, in 1998 only to lose because Scotty Nguyen was holding J♦ 9♣.

Julian Gardner made a Q♣ J♣ T♣ 8♣ 4♣ flush only to lose to Robert Varkonyi's full house on the river in 2002.

Best two-card starting hands to lose the final hand in the WSOP:

A♥ A♣--Bobby Hoff, 1979
A♠ A♥--Dewey Tomko, 2001

Appendix VI

NUMBER OF PLAYERS AT EACH WSOP

1970—38	1990—194
1971— 6	1991—215
1972— 7	1992—201
1973—13	1993—220

1974—16	1994—268
1975—21	1995—273
1976—22	1996—295
1977—34	1997—312
1978—42	1998—350
1979—54	1999—393
1980—73	2000—512
1981—75	2001—613
1982—104	2002—631
1983—108	2003—839
1984—132	2004—2,576
1985—140	2005—5,619
1986—141	2006—8,773
1987—152	2007—6,358
1988—167	2008—6,844
1989—178	2009—6,494

Appendix VII

1ST, 2ND, 3RD AND 4TH PLACE
PRIZE MONEY FOR EACH YEAR

1st Place	2nd Place	3rd Place	4th Place
1971—$30,000	None		
1972—$80,000	None	$20,000	
1973—$130,000	None		
1974—$160,000	None		
1975—$210,000	None		
1976—$220,000	None		
1977—$340,000	None		
1978—$210,000	$84,800	$63,000	$42,000
1979—$270,000	$108,000	$81,000	$54,000
1980—$385,000	$146,000	$109,000	$73,000
1981—$375,000	$150,000	$75,000	$37,500
1982—$520,000	$208,000	$104,000	$52,000
1983—$540,000	$216,000	$108,000	$54,000
1984—$660,000	$264,000	$132,000	$66,000

1985—$700,000	$280,000	$140,000	$70,000
1986—$570,000	$228,000	$114,000	$62,700
1987—$655,000	$250,000	$125,000	$68,750
1988—$700,000	$280,000	$140,000	$77,000
1989—$755,000	$302,000	$151,000	$83,050
1990—$895,000	$334,000	$167,000	$91,850
1991—$1,000,000	$402,000	$201,250	$115,000
1992—$1,000,000	$353,500	$176,500	$101,000
1993—$1,000,000	$420,000	$210,000	$120,000
1994—$1,000,000	$588,000	$294,000	$168,000
1995—$1,000,000	$519,000	$302,000	$173,000
1996—$1,000,000	$585,000	$341,250	$195,000
1997—$1,000,000	$583,000	$371,000	$212,000
1998—$1,000,000	$687,500	$437,500	$250,000
1999—$1,000,000	$768,625	$489,125	$279,500
2000—$1,500,000	$896,000	$570,500	$326,000
2001—$1,500,000	$1,098,925	$699,315	$399,610
2002—$2,000,000	$1,100,000	$550,000	$281,400
2003—$2,500,000	$1,300,000	$650,000	$440,000
2004— $5,000,000	$3,500,000	$2,500,000	$1,500,000
2005— $7,500,000	$4,250,000	$2,500,000	$2,000,000
2006—$12,000,000	$6,102,499	$4,123,310	$3,628,513
2007— $8,250,000	$4,102,981	$3,048,025	$1,852,721
2008--$9,152,416	$5,790,024	$5,403,352	$3,763,351
2009--$8,546,435	$5,182,601	$3,479,485	$2,502,787

RANKS OF HANDS TO WIN THE WSOP

Full House: 7
Straight: 9
3-of-a-kind: 1
2 Pair: 9
1 Pair: 6
Ace-high: 1
Jack-high: 1

MEMBERS OF THE POKER HALL OF FAME

Name and year inducted. See 1979 for selection criteria.

Nick "The Greek" Dandalos, 1979 (charter member)
James Butler "Wild Bill" Hickok, 1979 (charter member)
Edmond Hoyle, 1979 (charter member)
Felton "Corky" McCorquodale, 1979 (charter member)
Johnny Moss, 1979 (charter member)
Red Winn, 1979 (charter member)
Sid Wyman, 1979 (charter member)
T. "Blondie" Forbes, 1980
Bill Boyd, 1981
Tommy Abdo, 1982
Joe Bernstein, 1983
Murph Harrold, 1984
Red Hodges, 1985
Henry Green, 1986
Walter Clyde "Puggy Pearson, 1987
Doyle Brunson, 1988
Jack Straus, 1988
Fred "Sarge" Ferris, 1989
Benny Binion, 1990
David Edward "Chip" Reese, 1991
Thomas "Amarillo Slim" Preston, 1992
Jack Keller, 1993
There was no inductee in 1994 or 1995.
Julius Oral "Little Man" Popwell, 1996
Roger Moore, 1997
There was no inductee in 1998, 1999 or 2000.
Stu Ungar, 2001
Lyle Berman and Johnny Chan, 2002
Bobby Baldwin, 2003
Berry Johnston, 2004
Jack Binion and Crandell Addington, 2005
T.J. Cloutier and Billy Baxter, 2006
Phil Hellmuth and Barbara Enright, 2007

Duane "Dewey" Tomko, 2008
Henry Orenstein, 2008
Mike Sexton, 2009

Appendix IX

THE WOMEN IN POKER HALL OF FAME

The Women In Poker Hall of Fame was created on May 1st, 2007. Selection criteria are:

A candidate must have been active as a player or industry leader for a minimum of 15 years prior to election.

Player/industry leader must have contributed to the world of poker in some significant way. This person can qualify by either wining major poker tournaments, or by making significant contributions to the poker industry.

Player/industry leader must be a proponent of women's poker. Even if she does not play in women's events, she must support them.

The February 2nd, 2008 charter inductees were Barbara Enright, Susie Isaacs, Linda Johnson and Marsha Waggoner.

The June 5th, 2009 inductees were June Field, Jan Fisher and Cyndy Violette.

Ken Warren
Kennolga@yahoo.com